A SHEARWATER BOOK

LET THEM EAT SHRIMP

Let Them Eat Shrimp

The Tragic Disappearance of the
Rainforests of the Sea

Kennedy Warne

ISLANDPRESS / Shearwater Books
Washington | Covelo | London

A Shearwater Book
Published by Island Press

Copyright © 2011 Kennedy Warne

Library of Congress Cataloging-in-Publication Data
Warne, K. P.
Let them eat shrimp : the tragic disappearance of the
rainforests of the sea / Kennedy Warne.
p. cm.
"A Shearwater Book."
Includes bibliographical references and index.
ISBN-13: 978-1-59726-683-3 (cloth : alk. paper)
ISBN-10: 1-59726-683-3 (cloth : alk. paper)
1. Mangrove forests. 2. Mangrove ecology. 3. Deforestation.
4. Mangrove restoration. I. Title.
QK938.M27.L47 2011   578.769'8--dc22
2010043183

British Cataloguing-in-Publication data available.

Printed on recycled, acid-free paper ✪

Manufactured in the United States of America

10 9 8 7 6 5 4 3 2 1

Keywords: Mangroves, shrimp farming, aquaculture, wetlands, coastal development, storm barrier, marine ecosystem, environmental justice, Sundarbans, Tambillo, conchera.

The margins, on which the poorest and
most mobile had managed to subsist,
by taking advantage of the tolerance,
negligence, forgotten rules
or unquestioned facts, disappear.
—MICHEL FOUCAULT, *La Societé Punitive*

When I would recreate myself, I seek
the darkest wood, the thickest and
most interminable and, to the citizen,
most dismal swamp. I enter a swamp as
a sacred place,—a *sanctum sanctorum*.
There is the strength, the marrow of Nature.
—HENRY DAVID THOREAU, *Walking*

My heart belongs in the marshlands.
—PAT CONROY, *The Prince of Tides*

Contents

Preface

THE CRAB COLLECTOR squeezes through a tangled palisade of mangrove roots, lies on his belly, and stretches his arm full-length into the sloppy mud. With a grunt of satisfaction he draws out a mud crab that is broader than the span of his hand. Thumb-sized claws wave aggressively as he pushes the crab into a mesh bag that is already bulging with others.

He works his way along the shoreline, navigating the maze of roots that arch down from the mangrove trunks like umbrella ribs. He feels at home in these muddy thickets. This is his world, one he has known since childhood.

He realizes he is close to the perimeter of a shrimp farm that was built a few years ago behind the mangrove fringe. A hand-drawn skull-and-crossbones sign nailed to a tree trunk makes him nervous. There is no love lost between crab collectors and shrimp farmers. To the farmers, he and his kind are thieves, always watching for a chance to steal the "pink gold" that grows fat in their ponds. But it is the shrimp farmers who are the thieves, he thinks. They have stolen the common land and cut down all but this pitiful belt of trees.

He glances up at the watchtower and sees the guard, but doubts the guard can see him through the leafy canopy. He bends down once more to plunge his arm into the mud that gives him his livelihood. With a gasping cry he topples forward as a bullet thuds into his side. He clutches the wound and feels blood soaking into his shirt. He lies on the mud, pressing his body into its coolness like a child pressing into the arms of its mother.

He grips his hand around a root, trying to keep his mind from slipping into darkness. The forest seems distant and dreamlike. Above the blood singing feverishly in his ears, he hears the hoarse-throated frenzy of a guard dog, barking and barking and barking.

This is an invented incident, but it is not fiction. In mangrove communities throughout the developing world, crab collectors, cockle gatherers, charcoal makers, and artisanal fishers have been beaten, shot at, tortured, and even executed by shrimp-farm workers. In 1997, after two fishermen were killed by shrimp-farm guards in Honduras, Jorge Varela, the head of a Honduran mangrove-defense organization, wrote these words:

> Today, the artisanal fishermen cannot move freely across the swamps and mangroves where before they found their livelihood, for the *camaroneros* [shrimp farmers] have appropriated not only the land concessions granted to them by the government but also the surrounding areas. With the complicity of our government, we have given away our people's patrimony to a few national and foreign individuals, and we have deprived thousands of persons of their livelihood. We have turned the blood of our people into an appetizer.

This is a book about mangroves, but it is not possible to write about mangroves without also writing about the aquaculture industry, and especially shrimp farming, the single biggest destroyer of mangrove forests in the world. Were it simply a question of competing land use—forests versus aquafarms—perhaps it would be possible to shrug, lament the price of progress, and move on to other topics. But a great injustice has been done to the people who inhabit these forests and rely on them for sustenance and income. The industrial farming of shrimp on mangrove shorelines is not just an act of ecological piracy but one of social destruction as well.

So, while this is a book about the magic and mystique and magnificence of mangroves, it is also a book about the catastrophic loss of these forests and the damage done to the communities that rely on them.

To the people of the mangroves, *los pueblos del manglar*, I dedicate these pages.

Kennedy Warne
Auckland, New Zealand

Introduction

We suppose it is the foul odor and the impenetrable quality of the
mangrove roots which gives one a feeling of dislike for these
salt-water-eating bushes. We sat quietly and watched the moving
life in the forests of the roots, and it seemed to us that there was
stealthy murder everywhere. On the surf-swept rocks it was a
fierce and hungry and joyous killing, committed with energy and
ferocity. But here it was like stalking, quiet murder. The roots gave
off clicking sounds, and the odor was disgusting. We felt that we
were watching something horrible. No one likes the mangroves.
Raúl said that in La Paz no one loved them at all.
—JOHN STEINBECK, *The Log from the Sea of Cortez*

BY STEINBECK'S accounting, Weedon Island, in Florida's
Tampa Bay, might once have been one of the foulest places
on earth. An apparent wasteland in which nothing but mangroves grew, it resisted improvement. But in the bustling optimism
of post–World War II America, no land or person was beyond re-
demption. A rehabilitative program was undertaken. Weedon Island was sliced up as part of a statewide mosquito-eradication effort.
Trenches were dug to improve the flow of water from the bay
through the mangroves, giving fish better access to the wetland. The
more fish there were, the more mosquito larvae they would eat. In

a 1958 photo the island looks like a checkerboard, with each line a saltwater ditch.

But like so many ideas that involve human alteration of the landscape, there were unintended consequences, and for mangroves they were all negative. The spoil from the ditches was simply mounded alongside them, creating a network of dikes that were a few feet higher than the surrounding ground. Since the tide never covered these mounds, they were colonized by invasive species such as Brazilian pepper and casuarina pine, which subsequently spread through the wetland. The dikes and ditches also interfered with the natural surface flow of water—the slow, percolative trickling across the sediment that is the mangrove swamp's circulation system. An estimated 14 percent of Tampa Bay's wetlands died as a result of these earthworks.

Grand wetland-improvement schemes also left their mark on other parts of Florida. In the 1960s, canals were dug and roads constructed in the watershed north of the Ten Thousand Islands National Wildlife Refuge as part of a 230-square-kilometer (89-square-mile) real estate development known as Golden Gate Estates. The project was to be the biggest subdivision in America. It was designed in two parts, northern and southern. The northern tract was built; then the southern part went up for sale. Seventeen thousand people bought land in South Golden Gate. They were all suckered.

South Golden Gate has been called one of the classic swampland-in-Florida scams. It's become a standard joke: "If you believe *that*, well, I've got some swampland in Florida I'd like to sell you." South Golden Gate was that swampland, where, for years, real estate sharks showed gullible buyers the lots in the dry season, closing the deals before the land became flooded in the wet. Few houses were ever built, of course. The site became a haven of fugitives, poachers, and drug runners.

Is it any wonder that wetlands—but especially mangroves—get a bad rap? To anyone who hasn't explored them, mangroves are little more than impenetrable coastal thickets that cling to the edge of solid land and block access to the ocean. Just an obstacle and a nuisance. Which is why, not just in the development-crazed state of Florida but on coastlines around the world, they have been uprooted, torched, and bulldozed so that the land can be put to better uses. Mangroves are sacrificed for salt pans, aquaculture ponds, housing developments, port facilities, tourist resorts, golf courses, roads, and farms. And they die from a thousand lesser cuts: oil spills, chemical pollution, sediment overload, disruption of their delicate water balance.

Keepers of the dismal statistics of nature's decline say that in the past four decades, between a third and a half of the world's mangrove forests have been laid waste. These saltwater rainforests are now one of the most rapidly disappearing ecosystems on the planet. They are critically endangered or approaching extinction in 26 out of the 120 countries that have them.

The outlook for the next half century and beyond is no brighter. In addition to the existing threats, there looms a potentially more disastrous problem: rising sea levels. Standing as they do at the land's frontiers, mangroves will be the first terrestrial forests to face the encroaching tides. Spreading inland in sync with rising seas will not be an option in many places, for human development behind the mangrove fringe has cut off the line of retreat. Mangrove forests have become hemmed in on all sides, and the walls are closing in.

These are hard times for trees that are used to hardship. Consider where they live: rooted in the land and bathed periodically by the tides, they occupy a death zone of desiccating heat, airless mud, and salt concentrations that would kill an ordinary plant within hours. But through a suite of adaptations—snorkel-like breathing roots, a desalination system in their roots, props and buttresses to hold the trunk upright in the soft sediment, seeds that fall from the branches as ready-sprouted propagules—these botanical amphibians have mastered the art of survival in an extreme environment.

They don't just survive, they flourish. The forests they form are among the most productive and biologically complex ecosystems on earth. With one foot in the terrestrial world and one in the marine, mangroves support life in both realms. They provide roosting sites for birds and attachment sites for shellfish; hunting grounds for snakes and crocodiles and nurseries for fish; a food source for monkeys, deer, and tree-climbing crabs—and even kangaroos—and a nectar source for bats and honeybees.

In addition, they are breakwaters and land stabilizers of vulnerable coastlines, nutrient providers for marine ecosystems such as seagrass meadows and coral reefs, and a major contributor to the global carbon balance. And they provide homes, resources, work, and physical protection for hundreds of millions of coastal people.

Mangroves do not belong to any single plant family. They are less a lineage than a lifestyle. Their ecological niche is populated with some 70 species from 24 families. Among them are a palm, a hibiscus, a holly, two plumbagos, three acanthuses, a dozen legumes, a fern, and a myrtle. These sultans of salt range from prostrate shrubs to 40-meter (130-foot) timber trees. Though they reach their apogee in Southeast Asia, their distribution spans the globe. Most live within twenty-five degrees of the equator, but a few especially robust species have adapted to temperate climates, and one lives as far from the tropic sun as New Zealand.

Dispersed as they are across the globe, mangrove forests share one thing in common: they are among the most overlooked and abused ecosystems on earth. Why should this be the case, when they support such a wealth of species, perform so many services to the environment, and are relied upon by so many people? Why, as Steinbeck put it, are they so unloved?

Put simply, because they are misunderstood. Instead of being seen as wetlands of international importance, they are regarded as wastelands of no importance. They still evoke the old "swampland in Florida" prejudice.

This book aims to set the record straight. It explores the exceptional beauty of these ecosystems, identifies the drivers of their destruction, and shows how we might return them to a state of health.

Most importantly, it presents the human face of the mangrove forest. It celebrates the traditions that have evolved in mangrove communities and bears witness to the struggle those communities face as development interests claim a dwindling natural resource.

In these pages you will come to know the worth of a mangrove and the value of the rainforests of the sea.

LET THEM EAT SHRIMP

Chapter 1

Tigers in the Aisles

Mangroves are the supermarkets of the coastal poor.
—PISIT CHARNSNOH, *Thai campaigner
for coastal ecosystems and community rights*

HONEYBEES have been coming to the riverboat all morning, swirling about the decks and wafting through the companionways of the MV *Chhuti* as she toils toward the Bay of Bengal. Now and then one alights on my neck or arms for a lick of salt. It clings for a moment, then sails away into the shimmering heat.

I am three days into a journey through the Sundarbans, the largest tract of mangroves on earth. Shared one-third by India and two-thirds by Bangladesh, this vast tidal woodland is rooted in the delta sediments of the Ganges, Brahmaputra, and Meghna rivers, whose tributaries snake through the forest in a Medusa's head of silt-laden channels.

Rubáiyát Mansur, known as Mowgli, is my guide through the labyrinth. Lean as a jungle vine, with a gleaming black ponytail that stretches halfway down his back, he has been working on his father's riverboats since he was a boy. There was a time when he found the job boring. He worked with his Walkman headphones clamped over his ears, dreaming of escape to the city. Then the wild mystery of the forest began to seep into his consciousness. He began to notice the turquoise flash of a kingfisher's wings, the throaty cackle of a wild hen, the startled glance of a spotted deer. Now this world is his world, the life of the forest his life.

The bees' arrival tells Mowgli we're close to the honey section of the Sundarbans supermarket. Supermarket, lumberyard, roofing depot, fuel store, pharmacy—the forest is all these things to the people who live on its fringes. The Bangladesh Forest Department estimates that as many as a million Bangladeshis enter the Sundarbans each year to harvest its resources. An unknown number of these people—perhaps a hundred a year—do not return from their shopping expedition. Tigers prowl the aisles of this supermarket, where the shopper is also the shopped.

Mowgli scans the river for *mouali*, the honey collectors of the Sundarbans. Each guild of harvesters—fishers, woodcutters, thatch cutters, mollusk and crab collectors, honey hunters—has its own name and traditions. None of the workers live permanently in the forest, which has been a reserve since the 1870s. They enter it to earn their living, and in doing so they take their lives in their hands.

Mowgli spots the narrow, live-aboard boats of a group of *mouali* and signals the captain to nudge the *Chhuti* toward the bank. Half a dozen men emerge from a thatched cabin and greet us with broad, inquisitive smiles. Mokbul Mali, the leader of the group, tells Mowgli they are about to set out on a collecting trip, and agrees to take us with them.

A few paces into the forest, Mokbul points out a fresh tiger pug mark with his machete. The print is the width of my hand. Mokbul tears open a packet of cherry bombs and lights one. The explosion sounds loud enough to scare off any feline in a five-mile radius, but in this mangrove maze, one of the few remaining haunts of *Panthera tigris tigris,* the Bengal tiger, no one takes chances. Four honey hunters have already fallen to the paws of the tiger since the season opened a few weeks earlier. It is April, a month before the onset of the monsoon.

The men fan out through the forest, calling *"Ooooo-WOOH, " "ooooo-WOOH!"* to keep in contact with each other. Most wear an amulet for spiritual protection—a small metal cylinder with a scrap of paper inside containing verses from the Koran. They strap it on their upper arm or around their neck. Every few minutes Mokbul lets off another firecracker, bringing to mind Oliver Cromwell's dictum: "Trust in God, but keep your powder dry."

We push through thickets of young saplings, many of them a semideciduous mangrove called *gewa*, the leaves of which turn maple-red at this time of year. A gray lichen grows on their trunks. Mowgli tells me to scratch the lichen with my thumb. "Now smell," he says. I lean close and catch an aromatic whiff of aniseed, delicious in its unexpectedness. He tears a *gewa* leaf, and latex springs out. If this toxic sap splashes into a woodcutter's eyes it can cause temporary loss of sight, hence the tree's other name: "blind your eye."

In waterlogged areas the mud bristles with the pneumatophores—the aerial or "breathing" roots—of *sundri,* the tree from which the Sundarbans takes its name. The pneumatophores, 30 centimeters (12 inches) or more in height and as thick as deer antlers, grow so densely there is barely room for a foot to squeeze between them. The honey hunters scan the treetops for bees as they walk, but I keep my eyes on the obstacle course on the ground.

We enter a drier, more open part of the forest, where the soil is covered with a salty rime. Salt making was once a major enterprise in the Sundarbans. Seawater was boiled to make a concentrated brine, then poured into hundreds of coconut-sized terra-cotta bowls to evaporate. Earlier in the journey we had visited the site of an abandoned saltworks, where the ground was paved with shards of smashed pottery.

Mokbul considers this high-salinity area unpromising for honey and is about to turn back when a cry goes up—*"Allah-lah-lah-lah!"* One of the *mouali* grabs my arm and pulls me toward the sound.

Through the foliage, I glimpse thick folds of honeycomb hanging from a low branch. The surface is aquiver with bees fanning their wings to keep the hive cool.

Mokbul lights two torches made of tightly bunched mangrove fern, and we approach the hive. Bees hurtle in all directions, buzzing past our heads through the smoke. The men wear no protective clothing, just a piece of cloth wrapped around their faces. A *moual* with a curved knife gripped between his teeth climbs the tree and begins slicing off chunks of honeycomb and dropping them into a basket. He leaves a nubbin of wax on the branch to encourage the bees to rebuild. A comb may be cut two or three times in a season, Mokbul says, but by the third time "the bees will be very angry!"

He offers me a piece of the dark, dripping honeycomb. It is unbelievably good—warm, sweet, fragrant, with a kiss of smoke. There are about five kilograms (11 pounds) in the basket. The men hope to harvest a tonne during their month-long stay in the forest. Like most workers in the forest, they are financed by a moneylender who also acts as the purchasing agent. The *mouali* themselves cannot afford to make the trip without obtaining a loan to provide for their families while they are away.

Steps are light and spirits high on the way back to the boat. "We have preserved our honor," says Mokbul, beaming.

I have come to the Sundarbans not just because it is the world's largest mangrove wetland but because it is also one of the best preserved. That a forest the size of Everglades National Park remains largely intact and resource-rich in one of the world's poorest and most crushingly overcrowded countries is little short of miraculous. It is a tribute to the foresight of Bangladesh's colonial rulers. The British made the Sundarbans a reserve, imposed a strict management regime, and prohibited settlement within its borders—policies that are maintained today. Harvesters pay a fee to enter the forest, and there are set seasons and quotas for its various products.

Honey, timber, seafood, thatching materials, fruits, medicines, tea, sugar—the inventory of the mangrove supermarket is huge. You can even get the raw materials for beer and cigarettes. Each product is collected by its own group, or guild, of harvesters.

Of the many harvest guilds in the Sundarbans, none is more specialized than the otter fishers. One night the *Chhuti* passes a group of them sculling upriver as we chug down. Their boat is a dark shape on the dark water, the only light the orange speck of the oarsman's cigarette. Mowgli hails them, and we turn and let the two vessels drift together. Two of the fishermen come aboard for a cup of tea. The otters, housed in a bamboo enclosure on deck, squeak loudly for attention. There are two adults in one compartment and six pups in another.

During fishing, an otter is tethered to each end of the net mouth. Like aquatic sheepdogs, they round up fish, lobsters, and prawns that are hiding in holes in the riverbank or under vegetation and herd them into the net. Their reward is a share of the catch. The pups swim around freely, learning by watching their parents, and the fishermen pass on the technique to their sons in the same way. One of the fishermen says his otters once helped him catch a 40-kilogram (88-pound) fish, but adds that he thinks this fishing method may disappear. His own sons are not interested in carrying on the tradition. Mowgli says he knows of fewer than twenty villages where it is still practiced.

Not so the cutting of *golpata*, the mangrove thatching palm, which remains a staple Sundarbans livelihood. *Golpata*, or *Nypa fruticans*, to give its scientific name, is the only member of the palm family to have taken up the salt-loving mangrove lifestyle. Unlike most other palms, it does not have a trunk; its tall green fronds spring from an underground rhizome and stand like a feathery palisade along the water's edge.

Golpata has more to offer than just leaves for a roofing material. It also produces a sweet sap that is boiled to make molasses for cooking, used in skin ointments, and even employed as a snakebite medicine. In Singapore and Malaysia, *Nypa* fruits, known as *atap chee*, are popular as a dessert or in ice cream.

But thatch is the main product, and more than 100,000 tonnes of *golpata* leaf are harvested in the Sundarbans each year. *Golpata* cutters work in pairs, dropping the five-meter (16-foot) fronds with machetes, then ripping them lengthwise down the midrib by hand. They load the split fronds, odorous with sap, into skiffs and shuttle their cargo to a mother craft, a giant ark of a vessel that is stacked like a hay wagon. These tar-coated arks, the delivery trucks of the Sundarbans, move at an elephantine pace along the twisting waterways, propelled from the stern by a single massive oar. We saw one, weighed down beyond its limit with mangrove logs, which had sunk, leaving only the top of its cargo showing. The crew were on the riverbank eating their breakfast, apparently unperturbed by their predicament.

In the dense forest margins where the *golpata* cutters work, visibility is low and the risk of tiger attack high. Danger, however, adds no monetary premium to the product. A split frond sells for two cents. On a good day a man might cut a *kahon*, 1,280 split fronds, to earn $25. Like the *mouali*, the cutters wear amulets or scraps of red cloth that have been blessed by a holy man. They believe the Sundarbans to be a holy place, so they adopt many purification practices and prohibitions. Before entering the forest, they will not eat fried foods or uncooked onions. They will not comb their hair or look in a mirror. They always enter the forest with the right foot first and leave it with the left foot first. They do not work on a Friday, the Islamic day of public worship, because they believe the gods and goddesses will be too preoccupied with the prayers of others to protect them.

The superstitions extend to the cutters' wives at home. While their husbands are away they will not wash their clothing or hair, slaughter a chicken indoors, or withhold alms from a beggar. They will also not eat raw onions or burn dry chiles, believing that if they do so the aroma will be mysteriously transferred to their husbands, attracting a tiger.

At the beginning of the harvest season, the devout will make *puja* at one of the shrines to Bonbibi, the goddess of the Sundarbans, which are located around the edges of the forest. I visited one: a simple roof and walls of *golpata* thatch over a framework of mangrove poles, with a gorgeously painted tableau of the guardian deity and her attendants as the centerpiece. Bonbibi smiles benignly, seated on a tiger with a child on her lap. In some tableaus she has her pet crocodile at her side. Incense sticks and candle stubs are placed around her feet by supplicants. Her hand is raised in blessing.

According to the poetic texts, Bonbibi defeated her nemesis, the malevolent tiger god Daksin Ray, and offers her protection to those who call upon her. Her divine favor extends not just to forest workers. Many women regard Bonbibi as their mother and their goddess.

It is said that Daksin Ray, dark lord of the deep forest, can enter the body of any tiger and command it to do his bidding. I visited a forest department guard post where the staff had had to barricade themselves in an upstairs room when a tiger entered the building. The tiger climbed the stairs and broke down the door, forcing the terrified occupants into the rafters. At the same guard post I met a man who had been collecting firewood with three others when a tiger attacked. They were walking in a line in an open area near the buildings. The tiger sprang out of the forest and jumped the second man, knocking him to the ground. The third man tried to beat the animal off with a stick, at which the tiger turned on him, dragged him into the forest, and killed him. I was talking to the fourth man.

Even being on the water is no guarantee of protection from Daksin Ray. Tigers have been known to swim out to a boat and climb into it to take a fisherman.

Attacks on humans are more common in the drier, less lushly vegetated western part of the Sundarbans than in the east. It may be that prey species such as spotted deer and wild boar are scarcer in the west, leading tigers into greater conflict with humans. But the link is not proved. "Tigers are complex animals," Adam Barlow, lead researcher of the Sundarbans Tiger Project, told me. "We know so little about what makes them tick." Barlow's project, administered by the Bangladesh Forest Department, uses satellite tracking and long hours of personal observation to learn about tiger behavior and ecology—no easy task given their scarcity. A census in 2004 put Bangladesh's tiger population at just 440 individuals. Spread across the Sundarbans, that equates to one tiger per 1,200 hectares (about 3,000 acres).

To increase the odds of locating their study subjects, researchers use the controversial technique of live baiting. We stumble across one such bait station during a forest walk. It is a patch of raised ground that was once used by salt makers but appears now to be a tiger's banqueting table. Bones of deer and other prey are scattered about, and tethered to a tree in the middle of the area—a tree with deep claw marks in its bark—is a young ox. The animal seems preternaturally docile, as if resigned to its highly unpleasant fate. I can understand the researchers' rationale: by sacrificing a domestic meat animal, they might gain knowledge that could save a charismatic wild species from extinction. The goal is worthy, but the method troubling.

Mowgli points out a curious quid pro quo concerning tigers and the Sundarbans: the forest protects the tiger, and the tiger protects the forest. The ban on human settlement and hunting assures the tiger population of a large, prey-filled range, while the presence of a man-eating predator is a powerful deterrent for would-be poachers. The net result is a wilderness preserve in which unique human traditions coexist with healthy natural processes. A place that remains—as one translation of its name has it—the "beautiful forest."

Lately, tourism has come to the Sundarbans, driven in large measure by the chance to see a tiger. Riverboats like the *Chhuti* ply the labyrinth with nature lovers lining the decks, watching the unfathomable forest glide by. They come for a glimpse of the tiger, but, like me, many leave spellbound by a place of enchantment and surprise.

One afternoon I watch a bevy of spotted deer—antlered bucks, skitterish hinds, inquisitive fawns—drift through the red-leafed *gewa* groves. With their bright white dapples on roan flanks, they look as if they have stepped out of a Bambi film. Along the riverbanks they have nibbled the mangrove foliage to a neat line about two meters (seven feet) above the ground, as high as they can reach. It is as if the forest has had a haircut. Crabs, far from the tide, scuffle in the dry leaves. Woodpeckers hammer away in the canopy, halting momentarily in response to the shrieking alarm of a troupe of rhesus macaques. A wild rooster crows—an incongruous barnyard sound for such a wilderness.

A black-and-white butterfly, the rare Sundarban crow, floats through the saplings ahead of me, alighting like a feather on the twigs of a blind-your-eye tree. Under the boughs of a mangrove known as *kankra*, I stoop to pick up a green cigar-shaped propagule with a Tinkerbell skirt of sepals that has dropped like a javelin into the mud. As I reach for it I see two eyes watching me: a frog living in a mud crab burrow.

At low tide, with the prow of the riverboat wedged into a bank, I lean over the railings to watch blue-speckled mudskippers lunge and chase in the slurry at the water's edge. These amphibious fish, with goggly eyes on the top of their heads, are members of the goby clan. They "skip" on modified pectoral fins, and members of one species can even climb trees, using their fused pelvic fins as a suction cup. During their courtship and territorial displays they raise their dorsal crests like sails, violently flick their tails, roll in the mud, and blow bubbles out of their gills. They are truly bizarre fishes, icons of the mangrove world.

One night I sleep on shore, in a watchtower, lulled by the *junk junk junk* calls of nightjars, and wake at dawn to see deer tiptoeing out of the mangroves to graze on dew-moistened grass.

And always there is the dream of tiger. It is a local tradition, born of fear or respect, that the tiger's name, *bagh*, is not to be spoken aloud. To say it is to summon it. So on the riverboat we talk instead of *mamu*, uncle. "Any news of *mamu*?" I ask. And finally, one afternoon, we see him, taking his repose in the cool mud beside the water, fearsome and wonderful. Uncle tiger, lord of the Sundarbans.

Alas, no forest, however magical, is an island entire unto itself. Even a protected wetland like the Sundarbans faces threats, both from beyond its boundaries and from within. One is geological. For the last thousand years, the delta on which the forest stands has been slowly tilting to the east, causing the mother rivers that nourish the land with snowmelt and sediment from the Himalayas to shift eastward, leaving the western Sundarbans drier, saltier, and a less favorable habitat for mangroves.

Of greater concern than this gradual unleveling of the playing field is the diversion of water by Bangladesh's upstream neighbor. In the early 1970s, India built a two-kilometer-long barrage across the Ganges at Farakka, 25 kilometers (16 miles) from the border, to supply water to drought-affected agricultural land and protect the port of Calcutta from siltation. The loss of that freshwater input is believed by many to be the cause of widespread "top dying" of the majestic *sundri* mangrove, which can grow up to 30 meters (100 feet) tall. The topmost portion withers, often followed by the death of the entire tree.

India has another river-linking project on the drawing board, one that would create a vast spiderweb of canals connecting fifty-three river distributaries in an effort to move water from the rain-rich north to the drought-stricken south of the country. Bangladesh, the downstream underdog, views the scheme with alarm. Not only would it arrest the flow of fresh water, it would also choke the supply of vital sediments. The rivers that drain the Himalayas and sweep through Bangladesh to the Bay of Bengal carry an annual silt load of more than two billion tonnes—the world's largest riverborne sediment delivery. This sediment ends up as new land deposited around islands in the delta. To a country starved for land (Bangladesh's population density exceeds 1,000 per square kilometer, or 2,600 per square mile), this gift from the mountains is a great potential asset—if it can be stabilized before monsoon floods sluice it into the sea. Bangladesh has had some success in snatching the ephemeral drift of sediment. Over the past forty years, the forestry department has planted and stabilized 150,000 hectares (370,000 acres) of newly accreted "char lands" with mangroves.

Sediment trapping takes on even greater significance in a world of rising seas. In its 2008 report, the Intergovernmental Panel on Climate Change wrote that Bangladesh was "on course to lose 17 per cent of its land and 30 per cent of its food production by 2050"—a catastrophic blow for so populous a country. The coastal land is so low-lying that a sea-level rise of one meter would flood 14,000 square kilometers (5,400 square miles). Inflowing Himalayan sediment could never keep ahead of that kind of loss, but could extend the life of the Sundarbans and, in so doing, maintain Bangladesh's coastal barricade—its "green bastion," as it has been called.

Standing between the Bay of Bengal—a notorious breeding ground for cyclones—and the delta lands, where 40 million people live, the Sundarbans acts as a shield, soaking up the impact of surging seas. In 2007, the forest took the brunt of Cyclone Sidr, a category-five storm that made landfall on the eastern part of the Sundarbans at the end of the monsoon. Fishing boats were picked up and thrown ashore by the five-meter (16-foot) storm surge. Thousands died. A quarter of the forest was severely damaged. But without the mangrove barrier—150 kilometers (93 miles) wide at its broadest point—the scale of damage and loss of life would have been significantly greater. The projected reduction in freshwater and sediment input puts that guardian role in jeopardy.

Still another shadow falls on the Sundarbans. The rivers of the region are being stripped of their planktonic life by catchers of shrimp fry. As the sun sets over the Kholpatua River, on the northern boundary of the forest, I see an armada of banana-shaped boats stretching the full width of the river, each with a blue sock net anchored at the mouth and billowing downstream in the wind and current. The nets are made of mosquito netting, with a mesh size so small that all but the tiniest larval creatures are caught. The fishers work their way up and down the nets, thwacking them with sticks to dislodge debris, and every now and then checking the closed end for fry. They work the evening flood tide for six hours, wait six hours during the ebb, then work the next flood tide. We have arrived during the spring tides, when the current is strongest and the catch greatest. It seems that every inch of river has a net in it.

The fishing is all illegal. The government banned the netting of wild shrimp fry in 2000, but the law is universally unpopular and not enforced. There are not enough hatchery-raised fry to supply Bangladesh's shrimp farmers (many of whom prefer wild fry to hatchery fry anyway, believing they are healthier and more disease resistant), and the estimated 500,000 shrimp-fry collectors have few alternative ways to earn a living.

Out on the water we meet a former woodcutter who has been catching fry for fifteen years. The forest no longer holds any attraction for him, he says. Permits have become harder and costlier to obtain, and there are too many *dacoits*—armed robbers who roam the waterways as pirates. He owns no land and has a family to feed. It is a meager existence. Today, he has caught just eight fry in three and a half hours. "If God is gracious, I will catch more," he says.

Another fry catcher has his daughter in the boat with him. He is forty-five, he tells us, and has five sons and two daughters. He is afraid to work in the forest because he has a burst eardrum and is partially deaf. A tiger could creep up on him without him hearing, he says. From his fry sales he tries to put aside 300 taka a day (a little over $4) to educate his children. "Anything more goes for food, and tomorrow is another day."

Those without boats trawl for fry along the riverbanks, towing triangular nets that look like kites. Women and children wade in muddy, waist-deep water, pulling the nets first in one direction, then the other. Occasionally they stop to pick out the fry and transfer them to a round metal pot full of water. They put themselves in harm's way doing this work. Sharks and crocodiles have attacked fry catchers, and disease-carrying organisms lurk in these waterways.

Fry sell for around 300 taka per kilogram, numerically about 1,000 larval shrimp. In the morning the fry market in Burigoalini is packed with sellers sorting their catches, ladling a broth of darting fry into white enamel dishes to separate the different types—*bagda*, the saltwater shrimp, and *golda*, the freshwater prawn. Some shrimp farmers grow both types: *bagda* in the dry season, when the water in their ponds is brackish, and *golda* during the monsoon months of persistent rain. Others alternate a crop of shrimp in the dry season with rice in the wet.

As the *Chhuti* steams home to Mongla Port we pass an endless patchwork of ponds, called *ghers*, separated by low earth dikes and connected by canals to the river. We stop to speak to a farmer who has broken away a section of his pond wall to let in water at high tide. A grille of woven palm strips stops his fish and shrimp from escaping while the wall is down. He built his tennis-court-sized pond two years earlier, he says, and the income from seafood sales has enabled him to send all his children to school.

Who would gainsay this man's success? Shrimp has enabled him and others like him to climb up a rung on the development ladder. But for every person who has climbed a step by converting their rice field into a shrimp pond, a dozen more may have dropped down one. A shopkeeper in Burigoalini told us that a rice paddy supports a hundred people while an equal-sized shrimp pond supports five. "The other ninety-five have no option but to catch fry," he said. "Some have been reduced to begging." Conflicts over land use have led to sabotage. Shrimp farmers have breached the banks of saltwater canals to flood rice paddies, ruining crops and forcing the landowners to sell or lease their land for shrimp production.

But a back-to-the-land "anti-salinity" movement has also been gaining strength, and not a moment too soon. As vexing as the social issues surrounding shrimp farming are, the cost in marine life is appalling. It has been estimated that only 1 percent of the total harvest of the fry netters is the target species for shrimp aquaculture. Everything else is discarded and dies. The annual collection of wild *bagda* shrimp, believed to be of the order of two billion fry, is thus responsible for the destruction of up to 200 billion non-target fin-fish and shellfish larvae. How can the Sundarbans ecosystem survive this colossal slaughter?

If these are the troubles of a protected forest—its life-giving streams choked and diverted, an army of netters straining out its biological treasure—how much more vulnerable are the 99 percent of mangrove forests that enjoy no such protection? To find out, I traveled to Brazil, where, in the name of development, wetlands are being turned into wastelands, destroying a traditional way of life.

Chapter 2

Paradise Lost

A morte da floresta é o fim da nossa vida.
The death of the forest is the end of our life.

—*Slogan on T-shirt worn by Sister Dorothy Stang, rainforest martyr of Brazil*

FLAT-BOTTOMED PUNT with an ancient outboard motor ferries me across the Rio Jaguaribe. Golden light gleams on fishing boats catching the afternoon breeze in their sails. Laughing children dive like sprites in the river while a man fishes for crabs from a rickety pier. A straggle of mangroves lines the river's edge. Their looping, spidery prop roots make the trees look as if they have strolled out of the sea, found the place to their liking, and settled in. Who could blame them? The name of this place is Porto do Céu, the gates of paradise.

Two residents lead the way along a dirt track to show me their new neighbor, a shrimp farm. We climb to the top of an embankment and look across a patchwork of ponds to distant mangrove forests. An electrified fence stretches the length of the village and beyond. Skull-and-crossbones signs on the barbed wire issue a blunt warning: keep out. On the village side, goats mill about in grassless yards, cut off from grazing areas over the fence just as their owners have been denied access to their traditional collecting grounds for mangrove crabs, mollusks, and fish.

Even worse, the shrimp ponds have no lining, so salt water has percolated through the sandy soil and contaminated the aquifer beneath. The residents point to abandoned wells that until recently drew sweet fresh water to the surface. The water was *doce, doce,* they say, repeating the word as they savor the memory of its sweetness. Now it is *salgado,* salty, undrinkable. They have to fetch water from bores nearer the river or, if they can afford to, buy from the town across the river.

Outside a cantina on the beach, Manuel Ferrera Pinto vents his frustration. A fisherman for forty-two years, he came to Porto do Céu to live out his twilight years in this riverside paradise. But someone stole paradise and put in a shrimp farm. Now his well is saline, and he has no money to drill a new one. "They have made our lives a misery," he says. "All we have is what the environment gives us, but this they have taken away. I pray I have the strength to start again when the fresh water runs out."

Along the coast, in the village of Curral Velho, seventy-three-year-old Alouiso Rodrigues dos Santos stands in what used to be his vegetable garden. He has grown crops on this land since 1958—sweet potatoes, melons, cassava, beans. "We never had to buy from the market," he says. The land was so productive he had to tie up his papaya trees with ropes to stop the weight of fruit from toppling them.

In 2001, a shrimp farmer built ponds right up to the boundary, 30 meters (100 feet) from his house. Now, with the seepage of brackish water from the ponds, his land produces nothing but saltwort and weeds. Near the pond wall, the land never dries and is covered with an algal crust. Unable to grow food, dos Santos turned to the sea, borrowing money to build a fish trap. But heavy seas destroyed it. "The land threw me out to sea, and the sea threw me back to land," he says ruefully. "Where can I turn but to God?"

———

This is the *nordeste,* the sloping shoulder of Brazil that leans into the Atlantic Ocean just below the equator. It is a coast of heat-shimmering beaches, towering sand dunes, and cool, dark forests of mangroves. But in the past two decades it has also become a coast of shrimp farms. Zoom in on this landscape on an aerial mapping program such as Google Earth, and you will see the ponds where the shrimp are grown: hundreds of green rectangles notched into the dunes and salt flats and mangroves.

Indisputably, shrimp farming in Brazil has been an economic success. Between 1998 and 2003, the country sustained the fastest growth in shrimp farming in the world. Production leaped from 7,000 to 90,000 tonnes—95 percent of it from farms in this region. But the same ponds that have been engines of prosperity have been agents of social and environmental harm. They have displaced natural ecosystems and the human communities that rely on them.

To see the social and ecological footprint of the shrimp industry I am touring the *nordeste* with Jeovah Meireles, professor of physical geography at the Federal University of Ceará, and Elaine Corets, Latin American coordinator of the Mangrove Action Project, an environmental network based in the United States.

We set out from the city of Fortaleza before dawn, and by daybreak we are among the shrimp farms. Ponds crowd the landscape like rice paddies. Paddle-wheel aerators froth the water, and workers crisscross the ponds by kayak, filling feeding trays with fishmeal pellets. Fishmeal comes from so-called "trash fish"—non-target species—caught by commercial trawlers. It angers Elaine that not only does the shrimp industry destroy mangroves on land, but it pillages the sea as well. Between two and three pounds of feed are needed to produce one pound of shrimp. Depending on the proportion of fish in the feed (typically around 30 percent), shrimp-farming operations may be net consumers, rather than producers, of fish protein.

We stop at a roadside cantina for coffee and chewy tapioca pancakes, a favorite street food of Brazilians in the northeast. Jeovah speaks about the fragmentation of ecosystems and loss of biodiversity caused by shrimp farming. One of his research interests is the flux of energy between terrestrial and marine food webs, in which mangroves play a vital bridging role. "Shrimp farming sticks a dagger into that whole system," he says.

Jeovah has studied the Rio Jaguaribe and the communities it serves, including the settlement of Porto do Céu. He says that more than 40,000 people rely for their fresh water on an aquifer lying beneath dunes near the mouth of the Jaguaribe. The aquifer is a delicately balanced system. It consists of a lens of fresh water lying on a reservoir of denser salt water. The saltwater reservoir is replenished by the sea, and pressurizes the freshwater layer above it. The consumption of water by shrimp farms—16 million gallons per tonne of shrimp—throws the components of the aquifer out of balance, leading to salinization of the freshwater lens. Jeovah says that of the 129 shrimp farms in the area, 90 percent do not recirculate the water they pump from the sea. Most of the farms have no settlement ponds, but discharge directly into natural waterways—a recipe for environmental degradation. Small wonder that the villagers' water is *salgado*.

We walk along the embankment of a shrimp farm. Wastewater the color of antifreeze pours from a pond into a mangrove-flanked river. On the banks, fiddler crabs (called "hand in the eye" crabs in Portuguese) wave their Popeye pincers. They remind me of shipwrecked sailors, semaphoring the plea "Rescue us." Brazil's federal constitution states that all citizens "have the right to an ecologically balanced environment for the common use of the people," and that the government is required to "defend and preserve it for present and future generations." Yet such is the drive for development that new shrimp farm licenses are being approved all the time. Jeovah says 256 applications have been made to build new ponds in the Jaguaribe area, and, despite the existing environmental damage, not one has been turned down. *"Este é incrível,"* he says—this is incredible.

———

We continue along the coast, driving through towns with cobbled streets, tiled sidewalks, and pastel-painted houses with tall doors, wrought-iron balustrades, and flaking plaster—old Portugal preserved in her former colony. Jeovah has arranged to meet a youth group in a town called Icapuí to talk about ecotourism in mangroves. The group is keen to build a mangrove boardwalk and promote kayaking.

The mangrove area is near a fishing port. Fishers have beached their boats and are pounding caulking cotton into the joints between boards. The sound of mallets hitting caulking irons . . . a sound of the past. The boats have high superstructures, like miniature galleons, and workers on ladders and planks dip brushes into pots of vivid blue, red, yellow, and orange to freshen the paintwork.

Jeovah talks to the group about the mangrove ecosystem as we walk. He stresses the need for minimum disturbance when building a structure like a boardwalk. Mangroves are resilient systems, he says, but vulnerable to changes in water circulation. Poor planning could harm the very ecosystem they are trying to promote.

Despite the proximity of shrimp farms inland, this forest seems healthy. A carpet of seedlings has sprung up beside runnels in the sediment. Brick-red bristly legged *Goniopsis* crabs move nimbly over the roots of the parent trees. Against the dark brown of root and silt, they stand out like Christmas-tree ornaments. As if knowing what an obvious target they are, they retreat into clefts in the root matrix at the merest approach.

Seaward of the mangroves stretches an immense tidal flat, up to two miles wide. The stake fences of offshore fish traps seem to float above the sea in a mirage. Along this coast, where the water is shallow far out to sea, fish trapping was traditionally the work of *vaqueiros*, Brazil's breed of cowboy, who collected the catch on horseback. Curral Velho, the old corral, takes its name from those times.

Curral Velho is one of the communities in the northeast that has raised its voice against Big Shrimp. Villagers have organized petitions, challenged land sales, built a public information center, and published pamphlets. Some of the villagers speak out through art. One woman paints mangrove scenes for sale in Fortaleza, using different-colored mangrove muds as pigments. Another writes poetry to express her indignation at the destruction of mangrove lands. In the cool of the evening, when all Curral Velho comes outside to swing in a hammock or chat in a doorway, we sit under a mango tree while Maria do Livramento Santos recites a lament for the lost trees. Among the stanzas are these lines (translated from the Portuguese):

> Those who saw me before smiled.
> Today, those who see me cry.
> I am devastated, as if I were a lake whose
>   waters have dried up.
> As if I were a bird whose feathers
>   have fallen out.
> I feel the flames of fire rising in me.
> My roots are torn away from the trunk
>   by tractors.
> My leaves fall to the ground
> As if they were the tears that fall on the
>   face of a child when she cries.

Along the street, fish sizzle on a charcoal brazier and a man with a guitar sings sad protest songs. Someone hands me a pamphlet with the title "Crying for Justice." The cover shows a hand gripping a giant shrimp, fierce-eyed, mouth open to devour. This is how many people in Curral Velho see *carcinicultura,* the shrimp-farming industry: as a devourer of natural resources and livelihoods.

Sister Mary Alice McCabe, an American member of the Sisters of Notre Dame de Namur, is helping the community in its struggle. "One of the difficulties in fighting shrimp farming is that most Brazilians haven't seen it," she says. "They ask, 'Where does it happen, out at sea?' 'No, no, no,' we tell them, 'It is happening right here. They're digging up *your* mangroves, they're destroying *your* coastline.' We're trying to bring the story into the open."

It is no easy task, nor one without risk. In 2004, six Curral Velho fishermen were beaten and shot by shrimp-farm security guards for challenging the legitimacy of the farm's expansion into new land. In 2005, a fisherman in the state of Bahia was executed and his body dumped in a shrimp tank.

That same year, Sister Mary Alice's friend and colleague Sister Dorothy Stang was murdered in the state of Pará for opposing the illegal logging of terrestrial rainforests. The seventy-three-year-old nun, known as the Angel of Amazonia, was on her way to a community meeting when she was accosted by two men allegedly in the pay of ranchers. She was shot six times as she read aloud from her Bible the words "Blessed are the poor in spirit."

The forests may differ, but the same forces of dispossession are at work. In an interview after her friend's death, Sister Mary Alice said, "Dorothy was with the excluded migrant farmers in their constant, futile search for a piece of land to call their own. She pressured the government to do its job in defending the rights of the people." In the northeast it is subsistence fishers who are excluded—shut out of traditional harvesting grounds, protesting as the forests fall to the shrimp juggernaut.

Occasionally, there is a setback for the juggernaut. In 2005 an old whaling port called Caravelas, on the eastern seaboard a thousand miles south of Curral Velho, said no to the establishment of what would have been Brazil's largest shrimp farm. Elaine Corets was involved, and she wants me to meet some of her friends who stood up to the developers.

We drive there from historic Porto Seguro, the Bahian town that was the first landfall of the Portuguese in Brazil, in 1500. Today, looking at the line of old-style schooners at anchor in Porto Seguro's harbor, I wish I too could be journeying by sea, the way a coast should be seen, and certainly the way a town named "caravels" should be visited. One of the schooners has a for-sale sign on its rigging. It tugs at my heart as I sign the rental-car papers, opting for the road more traveled.

That evening, in the Caravelas arts center, Dó, Dedê, and Jaco Galdino, three brothers who work to promote the Afro-indigenous culture of Bahia, tell me the story of their town's brush with the aquaculture industry. Ten years ago, they say, it would not have occurred to them that the mangroves they grew up with could disappear. Mangroves were part of their life, as they were for most people in Caravelas. Then came the COOPEX consortium with a plan to build a 1,500-hectare (3,700-acre) shrimp farm on land between two rivers adjacent to the town. The farm would create 3,000 jobs, the consortium claimed.

For many in the community, the news was like water on parched earth. The 400-year-old port had fallen on hard times. Once a commercial hub for the region, Caravelas had lost its rail link in the 1960s, and since then both its population and its economy had declined. Widespread planting of eucalyptus forests on former agricultural land in the 1990s had forced even more people away. Shrimp offered a path back to prosperity.

But for subsistence fishers, crab collectors, and shellfish gatherers and their families, who lived and worked in the mangroves, the prospect of a shrimp farm the size of 3,000 football fields in their backyard was dire. They had already witnessed downturns in the species they harvested—perhaps the result of agrochemical runoff from the eucalypt plantations, perhaps caused by contamination or disease from shrimp farms farther north, no one was sure. This gargantuan new enterprise, displacing mangroves and discharging billions of gallons of wastewater into the estuary, would surely spell the end of their way of life.

Environmental groups were similarly alarmed. They saw the proposed farm as an ecological calamity in the making. The government had designated the Caravelas estuary ecosystem as an area of "extreme biological interest." Offshore lay the Abrolhos Bank, supporting the greatest marine biodiversity in the South Atlantic, the most productive fishery in the northeast of Brazil, and a budding tourism industry focusing on diving and whale watching. The mangroves and tributaries of the Caravelas River were known to be a crucial repro-duction and nursery area for species on the offshore bank. How could an aquaculture facility the size of the one COOPEX was proposing not disrupt those marine processes, they asked.

A clash of constituencies was in the offing. And it happened that someone in Caravelas had a professional interest in documenting the dustup. Cecília Mello, a social anthropology student at the Fed-eral University of Rio de Janeiro, had been living in Caravelas for a year, working on her doctoral thesis on politics, culture, and envi-ronment from an Afro-indigenous viewpoint, when the shrimp pro-posal surfaced in 2005. She dived into the fracas with diagnostic enthusiasm.

What struck Mello immediately was that the word "mangrove" meant something different to each group. To the consortium and the government planners who had approved the proposal, man-groves signified an untapped resource. To environmental groups, they were a vital component of the wider marine ecosystem. To sub-sistence fishers, they were home and livelihood. How could these groups communicate with each other when each was talking about a different concept?

The Galdino brothers saw what was happening: the groups talk-ing past each other, the war of words. They decided what was needed was an affirmation of cultural identity. It was not enough to be against a foreign encroachment. They needed to be *for* some-thing—to assert what made Caravelas and its mangroves unique.

They were already working with children from the community, teaching classes in everything from drumming to carving, silk-screening to sculpture. A fourth member of the family, brother-in-law Itamar dos Anjos, taught drama and dance. The brothers decided to explore the artistic possibilities of mangroves.

"We saw a need for cultural education to strengthen the idea of preserving the environment," says Jaco. "Instead of offering intel-lectual argument, we chose artistic expression."

Because mangroves and marine life were directly threatened by the

COOPEX proposal, the brothers decided to make a short film cele-
brating the spiritual and cultural significance of mangroves. *Não
Mangue de Mim* (loosely translated "Don't Mess with the Mangroves")
focuses on three *orixas*—deities of the Afro-Brazilian Candomblé re-
ligion—which are jointly responsible for mangroves: the goddesses of
fresh water (Oxum), salt water (Yemanjá), and mud (Nanã).

Watching the film with the brothers, I realize the vast differences
between the perceptions of those who live with these forests and
those who do not. The feeling toward mud, for one thing. To most
Westerners, mud is something to be avoided. In mangrove communities, mud is the walls of your house, the location of your food, and
the source of your income. Nanã is depicted luxuriating in it, smear-
ing her body with its cool, nurturing essence.

In the end, the mud and mangroves of Caravelas were spared.
Community opposition forced Brazil's federal environmental
agency, IBAMA, to reinvestigate COOPEX's application and rule
that the siting of the farm was an inappropriate land use. The project has now been abandoned.

To the brothers, the outcome has been not just a threat averted,
but a deeper vein of cultural identity reopened. "The shrimp proposal reawoke in the community the importance of mangroves," says
Itamar. But it also showed that many people had lost their connection to the forests. "Traditional knowledge has been lost, and that is
a cause of sorrow. Many Brazilians have only an economic knowledge, without respect for the environment. The Afro-indigenous
view is that nature is a single entity, with humans a part of it."

The Galdinos and their cultural group have been helping children find their way into that worldview. I watch Dedê tutor a boy
who is working on a mangrove T-shirt design. Outside, under an
awning, other children are honing their wood-carving skills. They
show me some of their completed sculptures of whales and dolphins.
The Galdinos teach the young artisans to use only dead wood. They
never cut living trees. They see their art as a way of giving new life
to dead timber, of reviving its spirit.

On the lawn a drumming session is in full percussive swing. When it gets too noisy, the teacher leads the energetic group down a path into the mangroves. The children march off, beating their drums like old-time soldiers going into battle. During her anthropological research, Cecília Mello found that, for children, mangroves offer a place of exploration and adventure, where they can learn to deal with the unknown. The forests become part of a child's "home ground," she wrote, part of the material and spiritual center of their lives.

That evening I meet two fishers who live a mangrove-centered life. Raised in the mangroves, they bring up their own children the same way. "Father to child to grandchild," says one, Genilson, aged forty-nine. His friend goes by the nickname Piaba, a type of fish. Genilson says there are 150 families around Caravelas who live in the mangroves. They don't have regular jobs. The mangroves are "their work, their business, their life."

These men are acute observers of nature. Their eyes light up when they talk about creatures they've seen in the mangroves over the course of their lives: fifteen-pound snakes, crab-catching raccoons that use their tails as lures. I had read about this behavior—how at low tide raccoons go into the mangroves, insert their tails into burrows and wait for a crab to latch on—but it seemed too fantastic to be believed. Piaba insists it is true, and delightedly mimics the yelps of a raccoon as it withdraws its prize. (One account notes that in this method of feeding, the raccoon is both hunter and victim—"a beautiful subject for philosophical musings.")

Some of the fishermen's stories cross from the natural to the supernatural. They claim to have caught in their nets the spirits of dead children, who refuse to show their faces. Piaba says that one night in the mangroves he witnessed a ball of lightning that pulsated among the trees as he watched.

The next day, Piaba takes us up one of the tributaries of the Caravelas River to meet eighty-six-year-old Seu Silvano and his wife. They live in a wattle-and-daub hut in which they have raised twenty-one children. Silvano came to the land as a young single man, cleared and planted it with fruit and shade trees, built the house, and says he will live here until he dies.

In 2005, some of his upriver neighbors sold their land to the COOPEX consortium. "They were crazy to sell," one of Silvano's sons tells me. Crazy because they knew what the farm would do to those who remained. "The effluent would have affected everything. Once it was contaminated, the river wouldn't have served anyone."

I ask Silvano if he still collects food from the mangroves, but he says his body is "too tired now." But he still knows how to sweeten crabs for market. As we walk back to the river, he lifts a wooden slat from a box under a mango tree. Several dozen blue land crabs, called *guaiamum*, scuttle away from the light. Silvano feeds them plantain and coconut to improve their flavor before his children take them by boat to the town.

It's a process that has been happening forever, down among the mangroves—and one that looks set to continue here, thanks to the creation of an "extractive reserve" on the Abrolhos Bank in 2009. The 100,000-hectare (250,000-acre) conservation reserve protects mangroves, estuaries, and other coastal habitats, but unlike many ecological reserves it has defined harvesting rights for local communities.

Brazil's *reserva extrativista* program—a bright spot against the country's dismal record of forest destruction—was initiated after the murder of rubber tapper and rainforest advocate Chico Mendes in 1988. Mendes pressed for recognition of the rights of indigenous people to extract natural resources from public lands. Today the more than twenty extractive reserves that the federal government has created are co-managed by an institute that bears the martyr's name. It was Chico Mendes who said: "At first I thought I was fighting to save rubber trees, then I thought I was fighting to save the Amazon rainforest. Now I realize I am fighting for humanity." Those who fight for mangroves may well say the same.

Chapter 3

Pink Gold and a Blue Revolution

The fishers also shall mourn . . . and
they that spread nets upon the waters shall languish.
—Isaiah 19:8

Endless Shrimp®—$16.99 per person.
—*Red Lobster Restaurants, November 2009*

SHRIMP AND MANGROVES. Mangroves and shrimp. The two are intertwined, ecologically and economically. They are like a pair of orbiting stars, though one shines at the expense of the other. The bitter irony is that without mangroves, there would be no shrimp. Mangroves are the natural nurseries of the shrimp species that are farmed commercially, just as they are for so many other marine creatures. In the wild, shrimp begin their lives in offshore waters, where the adults spawn. Then, carried inshore by currents, and perhaps aided by their own swimming, the larvae take up residence in sheltered inshore habitats where mangroves flourish. There, living and feeding in the shelter of the tangled limbs of the mangrove forest, they grow and molt until they are ready to migrate back out to sea.

Technology has short-circuited this ecological connection. Industrial shrimp hatcheries have taken the place of mangrove nurseries. From the viewpoint of commercial shrimp farming, mangroves are superfluous. And that is exactly what they have become on the ground. In most developing countries, it is not possible to visit mangroves without seeing the hobnailed bootprint of a rapacious industry. How did aquaculture come to be such a destructive force, and shrimp the mangroves' nemesis?

Let's go back to the origins of the industry. The oldest known guide to aquaculture was written in 475 BC and consists of advice from a Chinese administrator named Fan-Li to the ruler of a neighboring kingdom on how to get rich by culturing carp. The document contains information about pond size, stocking rates, nutrition, and predator control. (To ward off fish-stealing birds, writes Fan-Li, turtles should be deployed as "heavenly guards.") Follow his instructions, Fan-Li tells the king, and by the third year "the increase in income is countless." Aquaculture is pitched as a get-rich-quick scheme—just as it is today.

Remarkably, by the time Fan-Li's paean to piscicultural profits came to be written the Chinese had already been practicing aquaculture for 2,000 years, and today China is the world leader, responsible for two-thirds of global production. The industry has come a long way from the rearing of carp in ornamental ponds. Now dozens of freshwater and marine species are farmed, from tilapia to tuna, scallops to seahorses. Geneticists produce super-hybrid varieties that are disease-resistant and have faster growth rates, higher nutritional value, shorter life cycles (in the case of shellfish), and longer harvest periods (in the case of edible seaweeds) than their wild progenitors. Oceanographers scour the seas for microbes with potential for use as feedstocks, and aquaculture entrepreneurs design multistory "pondominiums"—whole cities of sea creatures.

Shrimp aquaculture (more accurately called *mariculture*, because most farmed shrimp are marine species) has a somewhat shorter history. It was not until the early 1960s that Japanese ichthyologist Motosaku Fujinaga, after thirty years of painstaking research and experimentation, succeeded in raising commercial quantities of the esteemed *kuruma* sushi shrimp, *Penaeus japonicus*, in captivity. Word of the breakthrough spread quickly, and Fujinaga's success was followed by further breakthroughs in hatchery techniques, feeding, and disease control. By the 1970s, farmed shrimp—"pink gold"—was the star of the Blue Revolution, the anticipated great leap forward in aquatic productivity that many hoped would rival the Green Revolution's surge in grain yields in the 1950s.

That dream has been realized. From contributing 8 percent of the world's seafood harvest in 1975, aquaculture now provides more than half. "Aquaculture ranks as a phenomenal story in global food production," says Jurgenne Primavera, a Filipino fisheries scientist who was named one of *Time* magazine's "heroes of the environment" in 2008.

Part of the commercial success of shrimp aquaculture arises from Primavera's own work on *Penaeus monodon*, the giant tiger shrimp, largest of the world's 2,000-some shrimp species, which attains lengths of more than 30 centimeters (12 inches) and a body weight of more than half a kilogram. In the 1970s, Primavera's groundbreaking studies on the growth and survival of tiger shrimp in the Philippines helped make *P. monodon* the most widely cultivated shrimp in the world.

It was only later that she realized she had a tiger by the tail. The industry she helped foster has bitten her own country hard, wreaking destruction on the mangroves that are a source of food and livelihood for millions of coastal dwellers. Between 1950 and 1990 the Philippines lost 66 percent of its mangrove forests. More than half of the losses were through conversion to shrimp ponds. A similar trail of destruction followed shrimp farming in Thailand and Vietnam.

"All across Southeast and South Asia, residential, agricultural and forest lands are being converted into shrimp farms," Primavera wrote in 2005. "Indian fishing communities who once were called *pattapu raja,* meaning kings of the coastline, now find themselves refugees of aquaculture development."

The damage didn't stop in Asia. As developing countries in the Americas and Africa staked their claim in the pink-gold bonanza, the mangrove decline accelerated. In 2001, it was estimated that aquaculture had been responsible for 52 percent of global mangrove loss, with shrimp farming alone accounting for 38 percent of the destruction.

The conflict between mangroves and shrimp farming arose from a simple geographical fact: prime pond location was in the shore zone occupied by mangroves. In its simplest form, shrimp farming involves building ponds in the upper intertidal zone, where mangroves live, and letting the tide fill them with water. This was the style of shrimp farming I witnessed in the Sundarbans. With the moon as a pump and the sea as a hatchery, there is little cost involved, but productivity is low.

As aquafarmers ratchet up the intensity, stocking their ponds with hatchery-spawned larvae, growing them with high-energy feeds and supplements, filtering, circulating, and aerating the water, and countering disease outbreaks with antibiotics, proximity to the sea, though not essential, is still an asset. Seawater can be pumped into the ponds from a short distance away, and transport of feeds and harvested shrimp by boat is practical and economical.

For the pioneering shrimp farmers of Asia and Latin America, there was an even more attractive reason to site ponds in mangroves: the land was available and cheap to lease. In most countries, tidal lands are state owned and cannot be bought or sold. Shrimp entrepreneurs found that governments were willing to grant them concessionary use of this land for peppercorn rentals. Governments were keen on shrimp because they were a desirable export commodity that brought in valuable foreign exchange. The World Bank and the International Monetary Fund promoted aquaculture because it helped developing nations diversify their exports and spread risk, and it kept the wheels of debt repayment turning. During the 1980s and '90s the World Bank, IMF, and other international lenders were enthusiastic backers of shrimp farming in the Third World.

The fact that mangroves occupied the preferred shrimp zone was inconvenient but of no great concern. The land was considered underutilized, and mangroves were easily removed. Predictably, any concerns about environmental damage were quickly overwhelmed by the irresistible force of commerce. The situation wasn't helped by the fact that jurisdiction over mangroves was often held by two or more government agencies with differing agendas. In the Philippines, for example, the mandate of the Department of Environment and Natural Resources was to protect and manage mangroves, while that of the Department of Agriculture was to promote aquaculture—at the expense of mangroves.

And so began two decades of concerted deforestation. Mangroves fell to axe, match, and bulldozer at a rate of between 1 and 2 percent per year—the same rate at which inland rainforests were being felled to make way for cattle and soybeans. It was a devastating double whammy for the forests of the Third World: slash-and-burn agriculture in the terrestrial rainforests, bulldoze-and-fill aquaculture in the mangroves. But while rainforest destruction quickly attracted urgent and vociferous opposition, the removal of mangroves was off the public radar. For most people, it still is.

Perhaps the most ecologically grotesque aspect of the shrimp industry in its early days was the practice of farmers abandoning their ponds after a few years and moving to new sites. A pond dug on a freshly felled mangrove forest receives a built-in nutrient subsidy in the form of organic matter stored in the soil. The nutrients boost plankton growth and increase pond productivity. But after a few years, the nutrients are exhausted and productivity declines. Wastes, chemical treatments, and unconsumed shrimp feed build up a contaminating sludge on the bottom of ponds, and if a viral disease should break out, future crops will be at risk in the affected ponds. Such problems can be solved with careful pond management, but with mangrove land undervalued, concessions cheap, and governments supportive or compliant, many shrimp farmers found it easier to cut and run than to stay and manage.

Pond abandonment is a double tragedy for the environment. Not only are additional mangroves sacrificed in the construction of new ponds, but the old pond land, rather than becoming available for agriculture or for replanting in mangroves, often ends up a toxic dead-end. Ponds can be successfully rehabilitated, but it takes time and money. So far, the shrimp industry has shown little inclination to address, let alone repair, past damages.

Aquaculture is often linked to the issue of human food security, and rightly so. As capture fisheries continue to decline, aquaculture has the potential to meet the shortfall. This has always been one of the tenets of the Blue Revolution. But shrimp aquaculture has never been about food security. Farmed shrimp is a gourmet product, not a dietary staple. It is, as Elaine Corets remarked to me in Brazil, "an exotic species farmed in ponds created by destroying local ecosystems and exported to wealthy countries for the consumption of overweight people who don't need any more protein or cholesterol in their diet." In the places where shrimp is farmed, food security does not increase, it decreases.

Shrimp-farm expansion in the developing world has been driven by a burgeoning appetite for shrimp in the West. Shrimp consumption in the United States nearly tripled between 1980 and 2005, while the price halved. Those decades saw a seafood delicacy unknown to the majority of diners become a ubiquitous item on fast-food restaurant menus and in suburban kitchens. Cheap price, availability, perceived health benefits, and high culinary status all contributed to shrimp's popularity. In 2002, shrimp elbowed aside tuna as the number-one seafood in the United States, and has held that position ever since. Americans now eat roughly four pounds of shrimp per person per year.

What most American consumers don't realize is that almost 90 percent of shrimp is imported, and two-thirds is farmed product, mostly from Asia. Diners, sitting down to a platter of grilled, battered, or breaded shrimp, wouldn't be aware that what they're eating is most likely a farmed commodity rather than wild fare harvested by shrimpers in the South Atlantic or the Gulf of Mexico. They wouldn't know that US shrimp-netting operations have been commercially kneecapped in recent years, unable to compete with the cheap influx of pond-raised product from abroad. And they certainly wouldn't know the backstory of shrimp aquaculture: the lost forests, the displaced lives. Advocacy groups are beginning to bring those stories to the fore, as they are with the entire industrial food chain, encouraging consumers to consider the provenance of their food as well as its quality and price. As Michael Pollan writes in his best-selling book *The Omnivore's Dilemma*, the questions we need to be asking are "What am I eating? And where in the world did it come from?"

The shrimp aquaculture industry claims to have put aside its destructive ways and to have embraced sustainability and environmental stewardship. The rhetoric today is of "greening the Blue Revolution." Of moving away from fishmeal to sustainably produced feeds. Incorporating traceability into the supply chain. Shifting out of the mangrove zone. Using a closed water-circulation system. Ending the use of antibiotics. Going organic. In the last few years, industry and environmental groups have been hammering out certification protocols in an attempt to bring shrimp farming in line with other sustainable fisheries.

The head may be moving in the right direction, but shrimp drags a long tail. Codes of best practice have been around for a decade, but while the market dithers on environmental standards, their adoption remains optional. Industry advocates may deplore ditch-and-switch pond abandonment, but along the remote coastlines of Third World countries, far from the eyes of consumer watchdogs, the practice continues. Mangrove wetlands go from being a multi-use public resource to a single-use private asset to a derelict waste.

Scarcely addressed in the sustainability debate is the social cost of shrimp, paid a thousand times over by coastal communities whose mangrove-based livelihoods have been pulled from under them like a rug. Improved environmental practice is one thing; rectifying the societal damage done to communities like Porto do Céu and Curral Velho—the "aquacultural refugees"—is another. Mangrove advocacy groups in developing countries have denounced the current shrimp certification process as "absurd, illegal, and unethical" because it excludes the victims of industrial shrimp farming. Of what merit is sustainability defined solely in environmental terms, ignoring the social destruction, they ask. The issue of compensation isn't even on the table.

Despite the problems, there is hope that aquaculture may yet become an asset, rather than a liability, for the poor. That at an appropriate scale with appropriate technologies, investment, and governance, it will provide a path to sustainable development. Many coastal dwellers are skeptical that this tiger can change its stripes, but Jurgenne Primavera is one who is working toward such an outcome. Having helped lay the foundations of industrial shrimp culture, she now looks for ways to make mangrove-friendly, community-oriented aquaculture a commercial reality.

Other researchers are experimenting with mangrove-friendly aquaculture techniques in Vietnam and Indonesia, both of which have a long history of multiple-option land use. One approach, called the silvofishery model, integrates mangrove silviculture with aquaculture. Mangrove seedlings are planted in and around the shrimp ponds, with the aim of producing an eventual timber crop as well as periodic shrimp harvests.

As Primavera notes, the new approach is a tightrope walk between achieving ecological and environmental goals on the one hand and meeting economic and social needs on the other. But having seen the catastrophic loss of mangrove habitat during the boom years of shrimp farming, she now places her emphasis on the forests. "Success will be had on the day my grandchildren walk with me through these habitats, understanding their importance, appreciating their diversity, and captivated by their magic," she says.

I've been touched by that magic too. But one thing my journey among mangroves has shown is that it's just not compatible with endless shrimp.

Chapter 4

The Old Man
and the Mud Crab

What attracted me about the torrid zone was no longer
the promise of a wandering life full of adventures, but a
desire to see with my own eyes a great, wild nature
rich in every conceivable natural product.

—ALEXANDER VON HUMBOLDT, *Personal Narrative of a
Journey to the Equinoctial Regions of the New Continent*

HE IS AN OLD MAN and he has been catching *caranguejo*,
the mangrove mud crab, for thirty years. "So I am just a
beginner," he says, cracking a grin as he walks along the
path to his boat. He tells me to call him "Seu Manuel," Mr. Manuel.
He is going to show me how he earns his living.

I am in the Parnaíba Delta, on Brazil's northeastern coast—
the heartland of crab and crab-catching. Along this coast, up to
a third of the rural population depends on the crab fishery as their
main source of income. No one knows the exact number of crab-
bers—it is not a registered fishery—but there must be thousands
who, like Seu Manuel, step into the mangroves each day in search
of *caranguejo*. And that's just in Brazil. Across Central and Latin

America, crab catching is one of the economic mainstays of coastal communities.

In many ways, mud crab is to Latin Americans what shrimp is to North Americans: entertainment food and restaurant fare. Seventy percent of the mud crabs caught in Parnaíba go to Fortaleza, a city of 2.5 million in the neighboring state of Ceará, where crab feasts at the beach are a weekend ritual.

Like wild shrimp, mud crabs rely on healthy mangroves to provide them with habitat and food. But whereas one species has become an entrepreneurial target of the rich, the other remains an artisanal fishery of the poor.

Seu Manuel gets himself ready for work. He is short and bony, with a wispy moustache and a tuft of gray hair on his chin. On his crab-catching arm he wears a denim gauntlet up to the shoulder. A string around his waist—his "tool belt," he calls it—holds half a dozen short cords for tying up the live crabs, along with a canister of mosquito repellent. He carries a hook for reaching into the deepest of burrows.

He paddles his skiff across a muddy channel. The tide has fallen a few feet from high water, as shown by a film of mud left on the lowest leaves of the mangroves. We tie off the boat and squelch and slither through sticky mud the color of cement to the crab zone. Prop roots form a dense maze of interlocking arches through which the lithe Manuel squeezes himself, muttering quietly and stopping every few steps to plunge his arm down a crab burrow. He moves so spryly through the mangroves that I think of him as a Brazilian leprechaun.

Sometimes he softens the mud a little by treading it with his feet, then lies full length on the gray muck to reach up to his shoulder into the crab's lair. Sometimes it looks as if he is trying to insert his entire body down the hole. About half of the burrows he tests produce a crab. If it is a *fêmea*, it is returned to the mud. No females are taken by the collectors. As well as being smaller than the males, they represent the future of the fishery. Males, *machos*, are tied four to a cord, which is how they are sold in the markets.

After watching Seu Manuel work for a while, I let him know that

I would like to try. He glances at me with amusement, then points to a wet patch of mud beside a prop root and goes off to catch more of his own. I push my arm in, trying two or three routes past a clump of mangrove roots that block the way, then find the main hole, or *toca,* and reach down the full length of my arm. Nothing. The hole seems to go on forever.

I try another spot. The burrow entrances are easy to recognize once you know what to look for. They are saucer-sized depressions in the mud that look like small puddles. (Later, as the tide falls farther, crabs will open their burrow entrances and emerge to feed, but now most are closed over with a plug of mud.) This time, again at the fullest extent of my arm, I feel something prickly and twiggy at the end of the tunnel—surely the legs of a crab. I wriggle and twist my hand until I have whatever it is in my grasp and pull it to the surface, hoping that the pincers aren't in nipping range of my fingers. I have just seen Seu Manuel bring one up with a claw clamped on his finger. When he shook the crab off, the claw broke away from the body of the crab before it let go of his hand.

I look at the squirming lump of black mud and crustacean I have in my nervous fingers. It is a good-sized male. I maneuver it so I have it pincer-end out and show it to the *mestre.* "*Grande,* no?" I say in my pidgin Portuguese. The old man grunts and nods, a smile playing about his lips. He's seen it all before.

I catch another one, but it is a *fêmea,* so I release it with my best wishes for the next mating season. May it produce *muitíssimo* offspring and keep alive this colorful traditional fishery, this gift of the mangroves.

Ucides cordatus belongs to a large family of crabs that includes ghost crabs and fiddlers. It lives exclusively in mangroves and feeds on mangrove leaves, flowers, bark, roots, and propagules, with a little sediment thrown in for variety. One subspecies lives on the Atlantic coast, and one on the Pacific.

Mud crabs do not believe in exerting themselves unnecessarily.

They spend between 80 and 90 percent of their time inside their burrows, masticating mangrove litter collected during brief forays onto the forest floor. No doubt part of the reason for their reclusive habits is that they are a tasty target not just for humans but for capuchin monkeys, crab hawks, mangrove raccoons, and, when the tide is in, predatory fish.

As the tide rises, the crabs seal their burrow entrances and retreat for the duration of the flood tide. Later, when the crabs come out to feed and collect provisions, they will clean out their burrow entrances, only to fill them in again when the tide returns.

There is no shortage of crab fodder. Mangrove litter-fall in this part of Brazil has been calculated to be 16 tonnes per hectare per year. The crabs' preferred food is leaves of the red mangrove, *Rhizophora mangle*, but they do not eat them when freshly fallen. *Rhizophora* leaves are full of acidic tannins, which gradually leach out as the leaf decays. Eating yellow, semidecayed leaves is easier on a crab's digestive system than dining on fresh fare.

The habits of these creatures are known intimately to the *catadores de caranguejo*, the crab collectors. Later, I receive an impromptu lesson in their biology from no less a personage than the mayor of the nearby town of Luís Correia, who describes himself as "the king of crab." I meet him on a morning when power is out throughout the Parnaíba Delta. The *nordeste* has had torrential rain for a month. The rain has knocked out infrastructure and made tens of thousands of people homeless. Fourteen have died. In Maranhão, the state that borders the delta, 40,000 are living in temporary shelters.

Luís Correia is a seaside town at the mouth of the Rio Igaraçu. Like many towns along this coast, it is a combination of fishing port and beach resort. On the side of town that flanks the river are dozens of jetties and fish-processing facilities. The ocean side fronts a crescent of surf beach with a string of open-air restaurants. In summer the beach is packed with bathers and kite surfers. Today the only beachgoers are a cleanup crew, loading trucks with debris washed ashore during the floods.

Mayor Francisco Araújo Galeno ushers Elaine and me into his office. Sweeping aside the needs of a town without electricity, he starts talking about what is clearly his favorite subject, the *caranguejo*. He was a boat captain for fifteen years, ferrying crab collectors to the mangroves, then set himself up as a distributor, and now operates two seafood restaurants as well. He speaks about the life cycle of the crab, about the three months they spend in their burrows waiting for their old shell to fall off, and how when they finally emerge their shells are as soft as jelly. Within two tides the shell hardens into the solid body armor a crab needs to protect itself from predators.

While we talk, the mayor's secretary brings in tumblers of iced water and tiny cups of hot, sweet *cafezinho*, the strong black coffee Brazilians favor. Fanning himself vigorously with a piece of paper, Galeno tells us about the closed season during summer when the crabs are mating. "This is the Carnaval for crabs," he says, "when the males and females are checking each other out—just as we do."

The mayor is exuberant. He speaks passionately about the role crab collecting plays in the life of the delta. It is the main economic activity of thousands of people, he says. He scribbles notes on a pad as he talks and gesticulates with his hands. I ask about shrimp farming in the area. Does the mayor find himself in a difficult administrative position, on the one hand protecting the mangroves where the crabs live (the source of his own livelihood), on the other encouraging new business activity such as aquaculture? He says that a recent slump in the shrimp export market has meant that aquaculture expansion isn't an issue at the moment. But he says Brazil's government needs to do a comprehensive study of the costs and benefits of farmed shrimp to establish once and for all if the economic benefits of aquaculture outweigh the damage done to mangroves and to economic activities such as crab collecting and ecotourism. His own position on the subject is clear: "Mangroves are our survival."

Glancing at the wall behind him, I notice he is flanked by a painting of Christ on one side and a crustacean montage featuring a huge stuffed lobster and a mud crab on the other. I ask if the "king of crab" plans to run for president. He laughs and throws up his hands. *"Deus sabe!"* he says—God knows.

Toward the end of the meeting, the secretary of fisheries, Luis "Rogério" de Sousa Filho, joins us and suggests lunch at one of the beach restaurants. Though it is the off season, we find one that is serving crab, and I go into the kitchen to watch how they are prepared. It's nothing fancy. The kitchenhand kills them with the stab of a knife, scrubs them under a tap, and cooks them in a pot of water. They are served with toasted manioc flour, known as *farinha,* and a vinegary salsa of tomato and cilantro.

We sit at rough tables under thatched sun shelters on the sand, smashing the crab legs and claws on the tabletop with a wooden beater and extracting the flesh with our teeth. The sweetest flesh of all is inside the carapace of the crab, where with each bite you have to spit out a mouthful of some sort of interior shell structure. We chase the crab down with Antarctica beer, served—as all Brazilian beer is served—*estupidamente gelada,* stupidly cold.

A roving seller of mangrove oysters—a species that grows on the trunks and roots of mangrove tress—comes past the table, and we order a dozen. He opens them with a short blade and drizzles them with lime, olive oil, and a few drops of hot sauce. We tip them into our mouths and enjoy their velvet smoothness. One more gift from the mangroves; one more reminder of the richness of these forests and the part they play in human lives.

Chapter 5

The Cockle Gatherers of Tambillo

Mangrove destruction is not only an ecological threat to a valuable ecosystem but also a social threat for [the poor]. External debt pressure on exporting countries, neo-liberal doctrines and ecological blindness of northern importing consumers, together with a flagrant lack of local governmental action to protect the environment in most shrimp-producer countries, are the main driving forces of mangrove destruction.
—Joan Martinez-Alier, *The Environmentalism of the Poor*

Nature or Pachamama ["Mother Universe"] has the right to exist, persist, maintain and regenerate its vital cycles, structure, functions and processes in evolution.

The State will apply precaution and restrictive measures in all activities that can lead to the extinction of species, the destruction of ecosystems or the permanent alteration of natural cycles.

Persons, people, communities and nationalities have the right to benefit from the environment and from natural wealth that allows well-being.
—*First, fourth, and fifth articles concerning rights of nature in Ecuador's new constitution, adopted in 2009*

*I*T IS HAPPY HOUR in Tambillo. On a shady veranda women sip soft drinks and play bingo, using dried corn kernels to mark the called numbers. Outside a cantina men slap domino tiles onto a wooden table, making each play as flamboyantly as if it were a game-winner. In the alleys children spin tops, flicking them down on the hardened mud, then scooping them up to spin on their palms. At the end of a long concrete pier—the most modern structure in this village of shanties on wooden stilts—a man is teaching his four-year-old to swim. He holds the boy in the water, then releases him to flail and laugh and splutter his way a few yards to the steps. The boy climbs up and flings himself back into the water and into his father's arms. Distant flocks of grackles scud across the estuary toward their mangrove roosts, flying just a wing's length above the golden water. For the people of Tambillo, this languid hour in the late afternoon is balm after the burning heat of a day's fishing or cockle-gathering in the mangroves.

Tambillo, in Ecuador's northernmost province of Esmeraldas, is one of the few communities where traditional harvesting from mangrove forests remains a way of life—which is to say it is one of the few parts of the country where shrimp farms have not commandeered the coastline. I have come here to experience something of the mangrove-centered life—a life that is disappearing.

I have another reason for traveling to Ecuador: this small nation sandwiched between Colombia and Peru was the first country in Latin America to climb aboard the shrimp express. I want to see the legacy of forty years of aquaculture. The broad outlines I know. Shrimp farming started in the south in the late 1960s and spread northward, displacing mangroves as it went. Labor was cheap, profits were great, destruction was rapid. By the early 1990s, half of Ecuador's mangroves had been cut down. In some places the loss was as high as 90 percent. In 1996 the 52,000-hectare (128,500-acre) Cayapas-Mataje Ecological Mangrove Reserve (REMACAM) was created to protect the last of Ecuador's great mangrove forests. The reserve includes a forest called El Majagual, south of Tambillo, which is reputed to have some of the tallest mangroves in the world. Twelve communities were granted the status of *custodias*, with between a few hundred and a few thousand hectares of mangroves placed under the custodial care of each. Tambillo, with about 600 inhabitants, is the largest of these *custodias*.

Yet, perversely, even within the REMACAM reserve forty-five shrimp farms have been built, covering 3,000 hectares (7,400 acres). Against the green-and-blue tapestry of mangrove and channel, the ponds look like cancer cells—cells whose malign influence extends beyond the ecological tissue they have already displaced. I saw the impact when I visited the giants of El Majagual.

They are remarkable trees. Though not especially broad—I could wrap my arms around the trunks of most of them—they soar to heights of 40 meters (about 130 feet) and more. The tallest tree ever measured here exceeded 62 meters, the General Sherman of mangroves. Prop roots spring in every direction from the trunks, the largest forming thick buttresses that hold the trees steady in the soft soil. Long wisps of lichen trail dozens of meters from the canopy, like trickles of water, and the roots and trunks are studded with bromeliads. Some were in flower—splashes of scarlet amid a hundred shades of green and brown.

The luxuriance is deceptive. El Majagual is not in good health, and may even be dying. In 1993 a shrimp farm built its ponds up to the boundary of the forest reserve. A channel six kilometers (four miles) long was dug between the farm and the sea to supply the ponds with water and to discharge effluent. This canal, along with the building of dikes, disrupted the hydrology of the area, depriving the mangroves of the tidal flushing on which they rely.

Florencio Nazareno, a guide from the nearby village of Olmedo, points at the mud beneath the boardwalk on which we are walking. It should be oozing and wet, he says. Instead, it has caked hard and is dry enough to walk on. Only the very highest tides now reach the roots of the trees. Because of the reduced saltwater flow, invasive species such as mangrove fern and strangler fig are taking over the forest. As we walk, Florencio slashes at head-high fern that has reached across the boardwalk and is blocking our path. The aggressive fern does more than restrict access; it shades out regenerating red mangrove seedlings that are the future of El Majagual.

When the shrimp farm was built, Florencio was one of those who opposed it. Like others in Olmedo, which has custodianship of the Majagual mangroves, he understood the threat the farm posed. "For generation after generation it has been passed down to us that mangroves are our life," he says. "If you kill the mangroves, you kill us."

He participated in protests against the shrimp farm, including an attempt to block the channel—the farm's main artery—and for his efforts became a marked man. He fled inland to the Amazon, where he worked in an oil-palm plantation. Six months later, when he felt it was safe to return, he took up a job as a ranger in the mangrove reserve, though his main livelihood is still fishing. He feels sure that if the Cayapas-Mataje reserve had not been formed to preserve El Majagual and other mangroves in Esmeraldas, the forest where we are standing would now be a shrimp pond.

By boat, Tambillo is only 30 kilometers (19 miles) from El Majagual, along a sinuous inland waterway that reaches all the way to the Colombian border. But Edgar Lemos, a mangrove advocate who is traveling with Elaine Corets and me through Esmeraldas, has people to see in the port town of San Lorenzo, so we go by road.

Edgar has been working for the preservation of mangroves for more than a decade. The issues he confronts here are the same as they are everywhere else: illicit logging, shrimp-farm expansion, acquisition of public land by private enterprises, overfishing. A new concern is Ecuador's latest agricultural boom crop, the African oil palm. As we pass an oil-extraction plant, Edgar points to where trucks laden with panicles of palm fruit wait to unload. Not only does the highly fertilized crop result in mangrove-polluting runoff, he says, but it also requires less labor to process than coconuts and other more traditional crops, forcing agricultural workers out of work.

As well as being a mangrove advocate, Edgar is a fruit lover who can spot a rare variety of banana from a hundred paces, so our trip is punctuated by stops at roadside fruit stalls. That Ecuador is the world's largest exporter of bananas is common knowledge, confirmed by the fact that in parts of the country you can travel for mile upon mile and see nothing but banana palms to the horizon. Indeed, Ecuador's southernmost province, El Oro, "the gold," is named not for the metal but for the fruit. Edgar is an aficionado of Ecuador's heirloom bananas, varieties that never see the hold of a container ship. Small, plump, thin-skinned, and bursting with fragrance, these yellow bombshells are a revelation in flavor, showing supermarket bananas to be tasteless imitations of the real thing.

As we drive, I ask Edgar about the narcotics war being waged along the Colombian border just a few miles north of San Lorenzo. He tells stories of cocaine kitchens in the mangroves, of drug shipments moved across mangrove channels by fiberglass submarine, and of the refugee problem. When the fighting intensifies, as it does periodically, up to 3,000 Colombian men, women, and children flee across the border and take refuge among the Ecuadorians. Edgar advises us to be cautious in town. The presence of gringos will not go unnoticed, he says. San Lorenzo has *muchos oidos,* many ears.

It is a drab, forgettable town, the most striking feature of which is a large sculpture of cockle gatherers in the main street. A barechested father holds a flaming torch aloft and marches toward a triumphant, no doubt cockle-filled future. At his side, his wife, carrying a basket of cockles, shares his gaze of destiny. A boy and a girl, also with cockle baskets, hold their parents' hands. The happy family stands inside a cockleshell, and the whole assemblage is surrounded by a wrought-iron railing. Traffic has to go around the giant cockle gatherers of San Lorenzo. It is gratifying to see humble subsistence fishers given this civic prominence—though the sculpture may unintentionally serve as a memorial to a vanishing species. In any event, these are the people I have come to meet.

We hire a boat and take a short, fast trip through the mangrove waterways to Tambillo. At the wharf there is a surprise—a realization that even a roadless village in a remote swamp is not as isolated as it seems. We are greeted by health officials collecting information about swine flu. Ecuador has just had its first confirmed case, leading the more sensational newspapers to run headlines such as "Pig Disease Has Fallen upon Us," as if it were one of the plagues of the apocalypse.

Once we have filled in the forms, Julio Velásquez, the director of Tambillo's fishermen's cooperative, welcomes us to his village and to his home. As he talks, I catch the words *manglares bonitos*—beautiful mangroves. There is no question in a place like this about the importance of mangroves; almost everyone here draws sustenance from the rainforests of the sea.

Before coming to Ecuador I had talked to Patricia Ocampo-Thomason, a Colombian who had written her PhD dissertation on mangrove communities in Esmeraldas. She found that almost 90 percent of households rely on fishing and cockle-gathering for their livelihoods. The two activities are usually split along gender lines: men fish, women (and frequently children) collect cockles. In Tambillo, three-quarters of the women are *concheras*. The shellfish they collect are of two species, known locally as *concha negra* and *concha blanca*, the black and the white cockle. Black cockles (by far the most common) live among the prop roots; white cockles live in more open areas of the mangroves. Both have roughly oval, ribbed shells that can reach eight centimeters (three inches) in length, but are typically only half that size. They belong to a family of mollusks called ark clams, so named because the shape reminded some ancient taxonomist of Noah's ark. Mangrove cockles are found between Mexico and Peru, and are the most commercially important shellfish on the Pacific Coast. Ecuador alone has more than 5,000 cockle collectors. In Tambillo the streets are paved with cockleshells.

After dark, I sit on a veranda listening to soulful bolero music pouring out of a nearby cantina, with the added percussion of a sheet of loose roofing iron rattling in the wind. The smell of frying fish and plantain drifts down the street. It feels good to be in a place where the symbiosis between humans and nature is strong. The mangroves nurture the community, and the community cares for the mangroves. The rhythm of life here is an uncomplicated beat. Work, play, eat, sleep . . . and tomorrow is another day. I recall something Ocampo-Thomason told me: "When I'm in Esmeraldas, I'm on mangrove time."

In the morning, Julio's wife serves cockle ceviche. The chewy meat of the cockle is marinated in lime juice and vinegar, then mixed with peppers, red onions, tomatoes, a large-kerneled corn called *choclo*, and cilantro. She serves it with lashings of the dark brown marinade, which is known as *leche de tigre*, tiger's milk. It is an invigorating start to the day.

After breakfast Aracely Caicedo, a *conchera*, comes to the house. She is twenty-eight, an Afro-Ecuadorian mother of four, a confident and eloquent woman. To begin with, she speaks about the demands and dangers of the job: the chafed knuckles and broken nails, the wasp stings and mosquito bites, the snake whose local name means "rot maker" because its bite can lead to gangrene, the stinging nettle that once pricked her in the eye, making her blind in that eye for a month.

Then there is *pez sapo*, the poisonous toadfish that lives in pools in the mud. If you accidentally step on this creature, you run the risk not only of getting a toxic spine embedded in your foot, but also of developing a painful skin infection from its eggs or slime. You can get the infection just by touching a root that the fish has been lying against. The preferred remedy is to sear the affected flesh with a hot knife or gunpowder. The *concheras* generally use gunpowder. Julio, who was a cockle collector for four years when he was a child, demonstrates the technique, producing a length of fuse and lighting it. I wince at the thought of young women like Aracely holding pieces of burning fuse to their or their children's skin.

Julio tells us he gathered cockles when he was between the ages of nine and thirteen, working six days a week (there is no collecting on Sunday). School was fitted around the collecting trips. He hated the drudgery and the fact that no matter how hard you worked, you couldn't earn more than what was required for that day's needs. The only good part, he says, was when the low tide was late in the day and the collectors camped overnight on the mangrove islands.

Aracely, too, talks about the economic hardships of her life as a *conchera*. There are regular costs to meet, such as rubber gloves, which many women use to protect their hands, waterproof (and toadfish-proof) boots, smoke torches to deter the mosquitoes (one torch is needed per day), and the boat journey to the mangroves.

Concheras rarely eat the cockles they collect. They can't afford to. *Conchas* are their only source of income. "Sometimes we pick mangrove snails from the roots, or we catch crabs," she says. But most of the time the women are focused on collecting as many cockles as they can for the limited time they have before the rising tide forces them off the beds.

They need a large harvest because they have many mouths to feed. "In this culture, women often have several male partners during their lives," Aracely says. "Children from those relationships always stay with the woman, so she may have to provide for a large family. A lot of single women with children are thinking, 'How will I get enough cockles to keep my children fed?'" The economic pressure is so great that pregnant women work right up to when the baby is due. One woman gave birth in the boat, she says.

The livelihood of a *conchera*, difficult at the best of times, has been made even more marginal by an influx of male collectors into what was once the domain of women and children. Traditionally, men fished or worked in agriculture or forestry. But declining fish stocks—partly the result of shrimp-farm expansion and pollution—have caused many to abandon fishing as a means to earn a living. Paid agricultural work, such as in coconut plantations, has also become harder to find as land is given over to growing African oil palm. So men turn to cockle collecting. But they work destructively, says Aracely. "They cut the roots with machetes and damage the cockle beds. Women work more delicately." Many male collectors are not from the local communities, and have no respect for customary rules such as leaving harvested areas fallow, she says.

On the cockle beds there is a mixture of cooperation and competition among the *concheras*. "The women sing back and forth as they collect—'one,' 'two,' 'three' as they find the *conchas*," Aracely says. This enables the collectors to know which of them has found the most promising bed. There's also a prayer the women make to the Virgen del Agarradero, the virgin of collectors, the *concheras'* saint, which basically says: "Let me catch the cockles first, and don't give them to outsiders."

I ask Aracely if there is anything she enjoys about the job. She laughs and says: "A lot of money in your hand." That fistful of dollars is getting harder to come by. The cockle stocks are in decline. A skillful *conchera* used to be able to collect 700 to 800 shellfish a day; now 100 is considered a good haul. *Concheras* receive less than 10 cents a cockle. They have to sell their catch to the boat operator who takes them to the cockle beds. One boatman may set the price at $8 a hundred, another $7.50, still another $7. The women cannot sell to the person offering the best price, because more often than not they will be in debt to one particular boat owner. Boat owners advance them money for boots or gloves, or tide them over with a loan if they or their children are sick or if one of them has just had a baby. The women find themselves drawn into a cycle of debt from which they cannot readily escape.

At holiday times such as Christmas, Easter, and Carnaval, cockles may sell for up to $20 a hundred in the cities. This bitterly frustrates the *concheras*, who receive only a fixed price for their cockles. "The price goes up and down for the consumer, but never for the *conchera*," Aracely says. Edgar wants to help create a community bank so that the women of Tambillo can improve their economic circumstances. Small loans are the key to creating alternative business ventures that will reduce the pressure on the cockle beds and help the stocks recover. A bank would also help the *concheras* have more control over their financial circumstances. Perhaps they could buy their own boats, or at least borrow money from a cooperative fund instead of going into debt to boat owners.

Aracely strongly supports this idea. In fact, she is running for office on the local council in the hope of improving the lot of the *concheras*. She doesn't rate her chances of election highly. It is expected of political candidates in Ecuador that they woo voters by extending various forms of largesse, and Aracely has nothing with which to buy votes. All she has are her dreams and her energy and her desire to see a better future for the children of Tambillo. "It is not good for them to start collecting as a little girl and become an old woman and be a *conchera* all their life," she says.

We fall silent, letting that reality, that sentence of inescapable destiny, sink in. In a few hours, when the tide is low enough, I will go out with the women and children to the cockle beds and see their work for myself.

While I wait, I walk around the village to see what is happening. A man is getting a close-cropped haircut with a razor blade. Some children are helping their mother make smoke torches, clumping strips of dried palm frond together and binding them with twine. Under the houses a motley menagerie of dogs and hens scavenge in the mud freshly exposed by the falling tide.

The tide is well out when women start to emerge from their houses, carrying woven cockle baskets and smoke torches down to the boats at the water's edge. There is laughter and the esprit de corps of an expedition about to commence, though this is an expedition many of these women have been making almost daily since childhood. School is in recess, so some of the women have children with them.

The boats are long, heavy skiffs called *pongos,* powered by outboard motors. Earlier, a smaller rowboat had gone out. Most collectors are willing to pay extra for a fast trip. The boatman checks off the names on his list as the *concheras* climb aboard. He pours cups of fizzy drink for those who want it, noting that down in his book as well. Eight cockles a cup is the going rate. When everyone is aboard, the boat starts across the estuary. The day is still and the sea calm, but I can imagine what this trip in an open boat with not much freeboard would be like in rough weather. Children sit in the bow. A young girl, maybe eleven or twelve, with wonderfully thick ginger hair spends much of the trip combing it. I look closely: she is wearing a string of pearls around her neck. Putting on the ritz to go cockle collecting.

Soon we are navigating ever-narrowing channels, ducking our heads under low branches, until eventually the boat can go no farther and comes to a stop against a clump of prop roots. Torches are lit and the *concheras* climb up the root scaffold, pushing their way into the forest. I join them, picking my way across the strong, springy roots, sometimes two or three meters (six to ten feet) above the ground. The roots branch and rebranch as they curve down from the trunks, creating such a jungle that getting down to the mud in some places is impossible. Once you are down on the sediment, you need to be a contortionist to move around.

I watch the women work for a while, then try my luck. It takes me several minutes to find a cockle. I show it to Aracely proudly, but she shakes her head. It is undersized. *Concheras*, at the urging of government biologists and in the interests of replenishing the cockle stocks, have agreed to a minimum length of 45 millimeters (about two inches)—though they grumble about the fact that their decision to forgo smaller cockles is not reflected in the price.

"We are being more selective and providing a higher-quality product, so we should be paid more," Aracely says. I can't see that happening. Where middlemen control prices, producers don't get such breaks. Especially these producers. Cockles are the fishery of the poor, and of women.

I notice that several *concheras* aren't doing much better than I am. I don't hear any of the singing Aracely talked about, the calling of the tally as each cockle is found. Today, I think there will be more praying than singing.

Chapter 6

A Just Fight

We, the "underdeveloped," are also those with the single crop,
the single product, the single market. A single product whose
uncertain sale depends on a single market imposing and
fixing conditions. That is the great formula for
imperialist economic domination.

—CHE GUEVARA

W HEN YOU LISTEN to the people of the mangroves, you
hear the voice of powerlessness and betrayal. By ceding
control of mangroves to shrimp farmers, the people's own
governments have stripped their livelihoods from them, sending
them this message: Your work has no value and your interests don't
count. When they protest, their words are dismissed as the ranting
of lunatics and troublemakers. And yet they continue to stand up
for their way of life and for the forests.

One step they have taken—small but significant—has been to
give themselves a name. In Ecuador they call themselves Los Pueblos Ancestrales del Ecosistema Manglar—the ancestral people of
the mangrove ecosystem. A name is an identity. A name is an affirmation of worth.

Another step has been to mobilize. In Ecuador, as in Brazil and
throughout Latin America, grassroots groups have sprung up to

protest the ecological piracy of the shrimp industry. I travel to the far south of Ecuador to meet Pedro Ordinola, the leader of an association of *cangrejeros,* crab collectors, which defends the disappearing mangroves of Huaquillas. At dusk we sit on the porch of his roadside cantina. His wife brings me a cooked mud crab that fills a dinner plate, along with a bowl of plantain soup. My conversation with Pedro is punctuated by the sound of my smashing the crab's shell and limbs with a wooden hammer to get at the flesh.

Pedro formed his association of *cangrejeros* in 2002 to protect the source of their livelihood from shrimp farmers. "I got tired of filing complaints," he says. "A complaint was like putting money in a corrupt official's pocket." He would file a complaint, an official would make a show of investigating it, the shrimp farmer would buy off the official, and the complaint would disappear into the fog of bureaucracy. In any case, by the time a complaint was investigated, the infraction was long past. "We were like a blacksmith pounding cold iron."

In Latin America it is common practice to name things—streets, organizations, children—after important dates, so Pedro chose 15 de Enero, January 15, as the name of the group. January 15 is the start of the annual closed season for crabbing. The closed season ensures the survival of the crab fishery. Pedro's association works for the survival of the crabs' home, which is their home also. One of the group's mottos is *El manglar es nuestra casa. Protégelo y nos alimentará.* The mangrove is our home. Protect it and it will feed us.

It is not just the physical destruction of mangroves that the group opposes, but the loss of access to a public resource. Barbed wire is strung through estuaries. Guard dogs roam the farm perimeters. Armed security guards fire at trespassers. "You can't get within five meters of a shrimp farm before they start shooting," he says. He shows me a map of the islands and estuaries near Huaquillas that shows changes in land use over time. Where there was an unbroken carpet of green in 1969, forty years later the red stain of shrimp ponds has engulfed the area. It is like looking at cemetery plots— which is ironic, since Huaquillas means "place of tombs."

"The *camaroneros*, the shrimp farmers, continue to gain title to lands that should belong to everyone. So we continue to oppose them. Otherwise the only way our children will learn about mangroves will be from photographs," he says.

In some ways, Pedro is an unlikely champion for mangroves. He was born in Ecuador's high sierra, far from the sea. A drought drove his family to the coast in 1978, when he was twelve. Even at that age, he says, he felt an affinity for trees, and realized that "when you lose a forest, you lose part of yourself."

Fronting an environmental group in a politically volatile Latin American country is not an easy road. He has had his share of death threats—all of Ecuador's mangrove defenders have—and a few bribes have been dangled in front of him, too. He was offered a second story on his house if he would stop obstructing shrimp-farm expansion. Money talks, but it doesn't drown out the voice of those who have been killed or maimed for asserting their right to make a living. "Usually they shoot to wound, to cripple, so the *concheros* and *cangrejeros* won't be able to work," he says. But in 2008 a *conchero* died from a shooting. The security guard who fired the shots claimed the man was stealing shrimp. The *conchero* was found to have 170 cockles in his kit, and no shrimp. In another incident, a *perro asesino*, an attack dog, was set on a cockle collector, and killed him also.

When I ask Pedro if he worries about his safety, he says nature will protect him, just as he is protecting nature.

Next morning, with Pedro's words about armed guards and attack dogs still fresh in my mind, we set out to look at the shrimp-farm invasion. We pay a few centavos and take the cockle collectors' bus to the port. Here, unlike in Esmeraldas, most of the collectors are men. At the port the tide is full. Skiffs are heading out with barrels of fishmeal and molasses—shrimp feed. On the banks of the channel, great egrets with necks so astonishingly thin you could encircle them with just a thumb and forefinger perch on low mangrove branches. This channel is the border, says Pedro. With just a few flaps of their wings, the egrets can be in Peru.

On the topmost branch of one mangrove, a pair of magnificent frigate birds preen. "Magnificent" is part of this bird's name—which seems a little unfair to other members of the frigate-bird clan, all of them strikingly graceful creatures. But then again, with the male's red chest pouch, which it blows up like a party balloon to court its mate, the angular jet black wings and the splayed tail that gives these birds the nickname "scissors of the sky," these birds are nothing if not *magnífico*.

A boat driver and a few members of Pedro's crab-collectors association join us and we motor to a patchwork of islands that lies off the coast. The mangroves fringing the islands are full of shorebirds roosting in the lush foliage, waiting for the falling tide to expose their feeding grounds. But all is not as it seems with these trees. They are a screen—a curtain that is one tree thick. Pull back the curtain and you find a shrimp pond. And another. And another. Stretching to the horizon. The impact is even greater on a satellite photograph: each island, gutted.

In 1978, a decree from Ecuador's National Forestry Directorate made it illegal for shrimp farms to be sited in mangroves. Yet here they are. By some estimates, 90 percent of Ecuador's shrimp farms have encroached on mangroves, and are thus illegal enterprises.

We keep motoring. Every few hundred meters is a gap in the curtain, and in the gap stands a shrimp-farm hut. In places, tacked to a mangrove trunk, is a sign with a skull and crossbones, and sometimes a crudely drawn machine gun for effect, and the words *Keep out. Armed guards.* Dogs pace the piers and bark at us as we pass.

We turn down a channel barely wide enough for the boat and follow the dike of a shrimp pond. Pedro stands on the bow, watching for underwater snags and pushing away the mangrove branches that crowd overhead. Every now and then he ducks suddenly to avoid the golden orb spiders that have spun their webs across the channel. You do not want one of these spiders unexpectedly plastered across your face. The females are a couple of inches long, and they pack a venomous bite.

We stop at a scene of desolation. Black stumps and branches are strewn over a wide area. The plot was cut two years ago for a shrimp pond. Pedro's association lodged a protest, and eventually development ceased, but only because the shrimp farm ran out of money. It was a rare success in the struggle against aquaculture incursions, but perhaps only a temporary victory. Trying to stop the site from being developed by another farm is an ongoing cat-and-mouse game. Pedro's group keeps an eye on this site and others, ready in case development starts up again.

The 2009 recession has given the mangrove vigilantes of Huaquillas something of a reprieve. So, too, has the fact that many of Ecuador's shrimp farms have faced outbreaks of a viral disease called *la mancha blanca*, white spot, which can destroy entire crops in a matter of days. When the disease first struck, in 1999, Ecuador was the world's leading exporter of farmed shrimp. Between 1999 and 2000, shrimp production fell by half and has never fully recovered.

While we talk, one of the men picks a handful of propagules from one of the living red-mangrove trees at the edge of the site. They hang from the branches like long green beans. Without saying anything, he starts pushing them into the sludge. It is such a simple act: you take a seed, you jam it into the debris. Come back in a year, it will have sprouted a pair of leaves. Come back in five, it will have become a shrub. One man sows destruction; another counters it with life.

As we drive the channels, I am struck by the depth of knowledge that resides in the memories of fishermen who have worked all their lives in these places. Such and such a spot was known for its large mud crabs; here was a place where cockles were especially numerous or sweet; this bay was renowned as a nursery for sharks. "Now if you set a net here, all you catch is mud," says José Ordinola, Pedro's nephew.

There is a wistful look in the men's eyes as they speak of mangrove stands they worked for crab twenty years ago, now either too dangerous because of trigger-happy shrimp guards or long since bulldozed and torched. They remember land in the center of islands that was cultivated for watermelon gardens and fruit orchards—now, like the mangroves, converted into ponds. Walking around the perimeter of one shrimp farm, we find crab pincers and legs mixed up in the dried mud of the walls. José can't resist reaching his arm into the mud at the base of the wall to see if crabs still survive under there. He finds one, a female, and beams. Even in this alien place, traces of the old world remain.

The ebbing tide grounds our boat. While we wait for it to float free, we quench our thirst with soft drinks and watch the world of the mudflat—a world of fiddler crabs endlessly gesticulating to each other with their arcane signals, of egrets wading with silent predatory intent, of whimbrels, oystercatchers, and ibises probing the sediment, of pelicans—*el pájarro viejo,* "the old bird"—floating in the shallows and then taking to the sky with grand, lumbering wingbeats.

Parts of the old world remain, but much of it is preserved only in the memories of old fishers. The Pedros and Josés, the *cangrejeros* and *concheros* of January 15, are doing their best to resist the decline, and doing so in the face of far-from-idle threats. When I ask Pedro what keeps him going—what makes him spend one more day standing up to a concerted and powerful opposition—he merely shrugs and says that *ójala,* God willing, he will continue the struggle.

At dawn on the morning of Sunday, July 26, 1998, several hundred men, women, and children from the villages around the island of Muisne, in the west of Esmeraldas province, gathered at the site of a shrimp farm that had built its ponds illegally in the mangroves. With them were activists from the Greenpeace ship *Rainbow Warrior.* Together, using picks, shovels, bits of wood, and their bare hands, they breached the dike of one of the ponds and let all the shrimp escape into the sea. Then they planted the pond with mangrove seedlings. It was the first time such a radical act of sabotage had been carried out against a shrimp farm in Ecuador.

Among the participants that morning was Líder Góngora, now president of Ecuador's national mangrove advocacy organization C-CONDEM. He tells me the story in his office in Quito, a floor above a restaurant called Martín Pescador, which his group operates. I poke my head into the kitchen on my way upstairs, to watch the cooks scurrying about like mud crabs, preparing seafood dishes for the lunchtime diners. Martín Pescador (Spanish for "kingfisher") specializes in the peasant food of *los pueblos del manglar*: fish in coconut sauce, mangrove crab, cockles on the half shell, a seafood platter known as ensumacado, ceviche, crisp plantain fritters called *patacones*.

Líder was born in the mangroves of Muisne. His parents were *pescadores*, and they were part of a community which learned that if its needs were to be met—health, education, electricity supply, clean drinking water—it would be through its own efforts rather than government initiatives. The villagers had watched with alarm as shrimp farms spread up the coast from El Oro. "They were like locusts," Líder says, "destroying everything in their path." Muisne was made up of cockle collectors, crab collectors, *carboneros* (charcoal makers), *pescadores*—all of them reliant on mangroves. When the first ponds were built on the island, the community formed an environmental group to protest the destruction of the forests. Even so, Muisne saw 80 percent of its mangroves disappear before it finally won custodial rights over the remainder.

In 2008, ten years after the dawn raid on the Muisne pond, there gleamed a possibility that Ecuador's long march of mangrove attrition might finally be ending. In a move that made headlines around the world, Ecuador's newly elected president, Rafael Correa, rewrote Ecuador's constitution, conferring legal rights on nature and the environment—an international first. The new constitution decreed that nature has the right to exist, persist, regenerate, and evolve, that it is the State's responsibility to prevent the destruction of natural ecosystems, and that communities have the right to benefit from environmental resources.

Yet even as Correa was receiving international plaudits for granting constitutional rights to nature, he authorized a decree aimed at legalizing the country's illegal shrimp farms. In exchange for shrimp farmers' cooperation in improving conditions for workers and funding mangrove reforestation, the decree absolved them from punishment for violating mangrove-protection laws and granted them ten-year concessions to the land.

Líder's group is fighting the legislation on the grounds that it breaks the very constitutional amendments the country just voted to accept, but he says that "dialogue with the president over the issue has become impossible." The rights of *los pueblos del manglar* and the agenda of the government seem irreconcilable. While communities like Muisne and Tambillo and Huaquillas receive the crumbs of custodial management of a portion of Ecuador's remaining mangrove forests, the *camaroneros* gain control of public land and receive a get-out-of-jail-free card. This under the regime of a socialist president who came to office in 2007 promising to distribute the country's wealth more equitably and, on winning a second term in office in 2009, reaffirmed "the supremacy of human work over capital" and vowed to stamp out the causes of poverty. "Nobody is in any doubt that our preferential option is for the poorest people," he declared. "We are here because of them. *¡Hasta la victoria siempre!*"

Some of those poorest are still waiting for the victory to swing their way. In 1999, when the Ecuadorian government first proposed that shrimp farms on state-owned mangrove lands be made the legal property of their operators, Líder's organization sent a message to international environmental networks, advising them of the coming outrage. The message was not a political analysis but a plain statement from a *conchera*. This is what she wrote:

> We have always been ready to cope with everything, and now more than ever, but they want to humiliate us because we are black, because we are poor, but one does not choose the race into which one is born, nor does one choose not to have anything to eat, nor to be ill. But I am proud of my race and of being *conchera*

because it is my race which gives me strength to do battle in defence of what my parents were, and my children will inherit; proud of being *conchera* because I have never stolen anything from anyone, I have never taken anybody's bread from his mouth to fill mine, because I have never crawled on my knees asking anybody for money, and I have always lived standing up. Now we are struggling for something which is ours, our ecosystem, but not because we are professional ecologists but because we must remain alive, because if the mangroves disappear, a whole people disappears, we all disappear, we shall no longer be part of the history of Muisne, we shall ourselves exist no longer. . . . I do not know what will happen to us if the mangroves disappear, we shall eat garbage in the outskirts of the city of Esmeraldas or in Guayaquil, we shall become prostitutes, I do not know what will happen to us if the mangroves disappear . . . what I know is that I shall die for my mangroves, even if everything falls down my mangroves will remain, and my children will also stay with me, and I shall fight to give them a better life than I have had. . . . We think, if the *camaroneros* who are not the rightful owners nevertheless now prevent us and the *carboneros* from getting through the lands they have taken, not allowing us to get across the *esteros* [swamps], shouting and shooting at us, what will happen next, when the government gives them the lands, will they put up big "Private Property" signs, will they even kill us with the blessing of the President?

One man who knows that threat—lives under the shadow of it—is Peter Segura. He had been in hiding for a month when I met him. His home is in Olmedo, where I stayed while visiting the giant mangroves of El Majagual, but it wasn't safe for him to meet me there. So he came to Quito to tell me his story.

Segura is an outspoken opponent of shrimp farming. He is, as Pedro Ordinola put it, "a stone in their shoe." When a powerful person has a stone in his shoe, he likes to get rid of it, which is why this soft-spoken forty-year-old Afro-Ecuadorian and his family have been hiding in the mountains.

From 1985 to 1995, Segura worked on shrimp farms. The work, he says, was difficult, dangerous, and low-paid, and the living conditions were spartan. Tasks included cleaning algal scum off the pond walls and water filters, keeping down weeds, dispensing food and agrochemicals, and hand-harvesting the shrimp. The workers handled fuels, growth hormones, and the preservative metabisulphite without protection. If a worker complained, he was fired.

Segura worked for farms in both Guayaquil and Esmeraldas, and came to believe they were operating outside of the law. Farms were supposed to be a maximum of 250 hectares (618 acres), he says, but by creating multiple subsidiaries a shrimp owner could achieve a spread of several thousand hectares. Many companies had politicians and councilors as partners or directors. The alliance of business and government "could do whatever it wanted with the laws, the ecosystem, and the people," he says. "I saw fish dying, mangroves being cut down, people treated like slaves."

In 1996 he renounced the industry and returned to his home in Olmedo. He started working politically on issues of health, environment, and community livelihoods, and this put him at loggerheads with the shrimp farm that had been built adjacent to the village. Segura claims that the farm ordered the destruction of community gardens, that its activities contaminated the village water supply and poisoned fisheries, and that it tried to exterminate green iguanas on the pretext that they were digging nest holes in the pond dikes and weakening them.

Protest action against the farm made him a marked man. Messages began to reach him, saying, "Take care or something will happen to you." Four times since 1997 he has been obliged to leave the community because of such threats. The threat to him is direct, but Segura believes the entire community is at risk. "The laws relating to environmental protection are explicit, but there is no institutional will to apply them," he says. "Big business can buy anybody off."

Segura's cell phone rings. It is a call from Líder Góngora. Segura greets him with the words *"Mi comandante,"* and for a moment I think of him as a modern-day Che Guevara, making his stand against economic imperialism. Líder had used the expression *"lucha justa"*—a just fight—for the battle to defend the rights of the mangrove people. And this is how Segura sees it, too. "My future is decided," he says. "It is to fight for mangroves and for the forcibly displaced families in the poor provinces where the shrimp industry flourishes."

Chapter 7

Bimini Twist

Negroes lashed in the coconut palms, ships blowing over the crest
of the island, two-by-fours sailing through the air like lances, dead
pelicans blowing by like they were part of the gusts of rain.
—Description of Bimini hurricane by ERNEST HEMINGWAY
in *Islands in the Stream*

Whenever Big Money goes up against the
Environment, Big Money always wins.
—PAT CONROY, *The Prince of Tides*

ANSIL SAUNDERS's boatshed stands open at both ends,
one that looks up the street to the King's Highway and
one that faces Bimini lagoon and across the water to a
long green smudge of mangroves on the far side. The boatshed's two
side doors are open as well, and a big fan whirs at full speed, labor-
ing to raise a breeze in the torpid heat.

On one side of the shed is a skiff at the skeleton stage, all
stringers and ribs, clamps and pots of glue. On the other side, when
Saunders pulls off the dust covers, is a finished boat whose lac-
quered sheen speaks of hours of patient sanding and generous applications of varnish and paint. The hull is the deep blue of oceanic
water. The deck and steering console and much of the interior re-

veal the rich red-and-blond grain of Bahamas mahogany, which locals call horseflesh.

The boat is for sale. It was commissioned by Bernard Madoff, Saunders says, but the deal fell through. The disgraced financier wouldn't be needing a boat where he was going.

Saunders picks up a big timber knee that has been roughly shaped into a bow stem and slaps it with his palm. "The hardest timber comes from trees that have faced the strongest winds," he says. He knows about strong winds, this man, fifty years a bonefishing guide and boatbuilder on this hook of land 80 kilometers (50 miles) off the Florida coast.

"We had a hurricane come through North Bimini in 2005—Hurricane Wilma. Winds of 100 miles an hour. Afterward I went down to the old Sunshine Inn, and the waves had split that hotel in half. Hurricane took that hotel and knocked its walls down. Boulders came up out of the sea, and the waves threw those rocks into people's houses. That hurricane destroyed concrete and steel. Then it went around South Bimini and ran into the mangroves, and it didn't do one iota of damage to houses behind the mangroves. Those mangroves tamed the waves right down."

Grand Bahama, an island to the north of Bimini that has no mangrove buffer, fared much worse, says Saunders. "That hurricane destroyed homes and raised the dead. Coffins floated right out of the cemetery." This, to Saunders, is the difference between having mangroves and not having mangroves.

In the old days, Bimini fishermen tied off their skiffs in the mangroves when a hurricane approached, Saunders says. "Those trees are not there by accident. They're part of God's creation to hold the land together. They save our boats, they save our houses, they save our land, and even when the water floods them they still do their job. They go underwater and come up green as grass."

Then Saunders tells me something unexpected about Bimini's mangroves. On two occasions he took Martin Luther King Jr. to a quiet spot in the mangroves of East Bimini to think and to write.

The first occasion was a joyous one. It was 1964, and King was working on his acceptance speech for the Nobel Peace Prize. Saunders took him to a shallow lagoon near a fishing spot called Bonefish Hole. There's a point in King's speech where he says, "I refuse to accept the idea that man is mere flotsam and jetsam in the river of life, unable to influence the unfolding events which surround him." I wonder if that thought came to him while he sat in Saunders's skiff in the mangroves.

Four years later, a very different King asked Saunders to take him back to that spot. He needed to gather his thoughts for a speech he was to deliver to striking sanitation workers in Memphis. "He looked tormented," Saunders tells me. "He knew the FBI was after him. He'd been told if he came back to the South he'd be killed. He'd been told that many times, but this time it got to him. You could see death in his face. He had often said he would never make forty years old. He was thirty-nine when he wrote that speech. He included his eulogy at the end of the speech, knowing he was going to die."

Saunders speaks the words of the eulogy—or at least a paraphrase of it—as if he were the one delivering it: "'On that day, don't say that I have a Nobel Peace Prize—that isn't important. Don't say that I have 300 or 400 other awards. I'd like someone to mention that day that Martin Luther King Jr. tried to give his life serving others. Say that I tried to feed the hungry, clothe the naked, visit those who were in prison. Say that I tried to love and serve humanity.' King wrote those words in my boat in the mangroves, and three days later he was shot."

The memory of King in the mangroves seems as fresh to Saunders as if the man had just visited. "Birds overhead, tide trickling by, grunts and snappers running under the mangrove roots, stingray burying and reburying in the sand. At one point King said to me, 'There's so much life all around us here—how could people see all this and not believe in God?' Today I call that spot holy ground."

Saunders is wearing an Obama '08 baseball cap. I'm glad this seventy-six-year-old Biminite lived to see a day that showed King's work was not in vain.

A golf cart takes me back through Alice Town to the pier. I stop at a diner for a plate of conch salad (locals pronounce it "conk") and a slice of banana bread, and listen to the lunchtime conversations in Bahamian creole. I can barely understand a word, but the Caribbean cadence is beguiling. The white-fleshed conch meat is a local delicacy, and the big empty shells, with their blush-pink nacreous interior and knuckle-studded exterior, are Bimini's ubiquitous landscaping feature. They line paths and driveways and encircle the bases of palm trees, and broken fragments are embedded in the tops of walls to deter burglars. You can slide your hand inside the mouth of the shell and grip it on your fist—hence the nickname "Bimini boxing glove."

Bimini was Hemingway's stomping ground in the 1930s. He drank Green Isaacs at the Compleat Angler Hotel (since burned down, incinerating a wealth of memorabilia with it) and fished for marlin and sailfish in the Gulf Stream. His celebrity and fishing prowess helped establish Bimini as an angler's El Dorado. It is still known as the bonefishing capital of the world.

Hemingway hated sharks. Perhaps not more than any angler of his day, though few would have employed his method of dispatching them: spraying them with bullets. In an episode in his novel *Islands in the Stream*, a thousand-pound hammerhead lunges through a gap in the Bimini reef toward a group of spearfishing children. The great fish, "his yard-wide mouth like a turned-up grin," is stopped by the deckhand's tommy gun "rapping and ripping into the white of his belly making black spots that were red before he turned and went down." The story is fiction, but the bloodshed was standard practice. Once, while Hemingway was patrolling for U-boats during World War II in his launch *Pilar*, his deckhand tossed a grenade into the mouth of a hooked mako. On another occasion, angry that the fish he had brought to the boat after a long battle turned out to be a tiger shark and not a marlin, Hemingway shot his initials into its head. Hemingway was Quint before Quint was invented, before *Jaws* made shark fear and loathing part of the cultural narrative.

So I find it pleasingly ironic that Bimini is now a center for shark research, conservation, and advocacy. Tour groups visiting the Bimini Biological Field Station, aka Shark Lab, learn that sharks are not death fish from hell but some of the smartest, most highly specialized animals in the ocean, and some of the most ruthlessly overfished and endangered. A poster of a mako on the wall of the lab cuts to the heart of the shark-finning tragedy—the destruction of sharks for the sole purpose of supplying an ingredient in Asian soup. The wording reads: "For 400 million years the undisputed lord of the oceans. Now presiding over four ounces of tepid broth and a mushroom."

Shark Lab is owned and directed by Miami marine biologist Samuel Gruber, a world authority on shark behavior and ecology. In a twist that Hemingway would have appreciated, it was an encounter with an aggressive hammerhead while spearfishing that spurred the teenage Gruber to devote his life to studying sharks. "I was absolutely terrified and awed, yet the giant fish was beautiful, magnificent, and was circling me," Gruber recalled. "When it did not actually kill and consume me, I knew that I wanted to learn more about these splendid creatures."

Gruber's main research focus has been lemon sharks, a tropical species whose juveniles spend their first few years in the protective confines of mangroves. His first research sites were in the Florida Keys, but by the early 1980s environmental stresses and overfishing had caused the population to plummet. "Fewer and fewer adult sharks were coming back to give birth," he told me when I visited him in Miami. "In 1984 we had to abandon the study because we weren't getting any more baby sharks."

Gruber looked around the Bahamas for an alternative research site and eventually chose Bimini. It was handy to Florida, close to the Gulf Stream (a known shark corridor), and had a relatively pristine marine environment, with good numbers of mangroves and lemon sharks. After several years of visiting the islands for summer fieldwork, in 1990 he decided to open a permanent facility. Two decades on, the lab continues to provide a rare glimpse into the ways of sharks, traditionally among the ocean's most difficult animals to study.

In the 1970s and early '80s Gruber's research focus was bioenergetics, a branch of biology that studies energy flow through living systems. He and his colleagues measured lemon sharks' food intake and metabolic rate and looked at how food energy was partitioned in the body. "This work gave us basic information on how an individual shark functions," he said. In Bimini, he turned his attention to the population as a whole, using techniques such as satellite tracking and DNA profiling to find out how the sharks interact with each other and with their environment. The results, he says, have been "a revolution in our understanding of how sharks work."

The population study has been running for fifteen years. A key part of the fieldwork is an annual lemon-shark census, during which volunteers from around the world help the Shark Lab's resident researchers catch all the juvenile sharks in the main nursery areas in the lagoon. The census is one of the reasons I've come to Bimini.

Lemon sharks belong to the family of requiem sharks, all of which bear live young. The pups are born in spring, and there are usually about ten in a litter—though not all have the same father. The Bimini research has shown that a single litter can be sired by up to four males. The pups live in and around the mangroves, eating fish, crabs, crawfish, and octopus, until they reach a little over three feet in length and are becoming less vulnerable to predators (typically larger sharks, including members of their own species). The adolescent sharks then move into deeper, more exposed waters. Some remain near Bimini and some move away, perhaps to other islands in the Bahamas, perhaps farther afield; no one is sure. Females start to return to Bimini when they are sexually mature, around twelve years old, giving birth in exactly the same place they themselves were born. Males almost never return to their natal island—the lemon shark's way of avoiding inbreeding.

It's mid-June, and the census is in full swing. I join the lab's director, Bryan Franks, on a boat run out to the middle of the lagoon, where all the sharks they've caught so far this year are corralled in a makeshift pen. Franks is going to perform a stomach eversion on a shark caught the previous evening. It's a newborn about two feet long, swimming in a small holding pen next to the main one. He anesthetizes it, then gently pulls the animal's stomach through its mouth and removes a few fragments of undigested fish from inside it. The procedure, which sounds more drastic than it actually is, takes only a few minutes, and afterward the shark is released into the pen with the others. The stomach contents will be analyzed as part of a study to test the theory that sharks play an important ecological role in culling weak and sick animals from prey populations.

We put on masks and snorkels and climb into the main pen to check that all the sharks are healthy and swimming strongly. There are more than a hundred in here. They are lean and sinuous—greyhounds of the shark world—charcoal gray on top and white underneath, methodically circling the plastic mesh walls of the pen. If I swim in the opposite direction, they stream past me like cars on a freeway. Pens are set up in each of the census areas to ensure that sharks aren't caught more than once. As soon as all the juveniles have been captured (the researchers estimate a 99 percent capture rate), they are released.

A couple of hours before sunset, I join one of the boat crews for a night of shark catching. The work happens at night because that is when the sharks are most active, venturing out from the safety of the mangrove nursery into the open water of the seagrass flats. The teams motor out to the edge of a swathe of virgin mangroves and set their gillnets, tying one end to a mangrove trunk and the other to a pole sunk into the sediment. The lagoon here is shallow, no more than about knee-deep, except for soft spots where without warning you sink to your waist. That's no hardship: the water is bathtub warm. Every fifteen minutes, two crew members walk the length of the 100-meter net. If they find a shark it is whisked away to a centrally located tagging boat to be weighed, measured, and, if it is a newborn, injected with an electronic tag that can be read with a scanner, like a bar code. All of the captured sharks are weighed, measured, and sexed, and a nick of tissue is taken from the base of the dorsal fin for DNA analysis. They are then released into the holding pen.

It's a slow night. Most walks of the net yield nothing. This nursery area has been netted on the two previous nights, and two-thirds of the juveniles have already been captured. Even so, our team is elated to catch four in the space of five hours.

There's a lot of bonhomie out on the water. The net crews are constantly on the radio, congratulating each other on a capture, ribbing each other if they're not catching anything, sharing snatches of songs from their iPods, posing obscure trivia questions (one of the catchers happens to be an expert on *Pirates of the Caribbean*). Our boat is near a derelict concrete structure that is a favorite spot for mating stingrays. We hear loud splashings as the big animals engage in their amorous assignations.

The two dozen census volunteers come from as far afield as the United Kingdom and Holland to spend a sleep-deprived month swatting mosquitoes and being drenched by tropical rainstorms for the shark cause. Some come back year after year, and they pay for the privilege. I ask the crew in my boat if it's the sharks or the camaraderie that draws them here. With one voice they say: "The sharks!" These young sharkophiles are helping to rewrite the shark narrative—an enterprise long overdue and, for some shark species, possibly too late.

In 1997, Gruber learned that a developer was planning to build a mega-resort on a 300-hectare (741-acre) property that covered much of the northern end of Bimini, including some of the islands' finest mangrove areas. Alarm bells started to ring. He had had to abandon his Florida Keys site; was history about to repeat itself?

"I got wind of the project when the developer sent a team to produce a so-called environmental impact statement," Gruber told me. "They came to see me and told me their plans, and I said, 'You can't do that. You can't pull out all these mangroves and do all this dredging. You'll destroy the whole island ecology.' The developer wanted to remove mangroves and build a golf course, two hotels, two marinas, a 10,000-square-foot casino, a 5,000-foot airstrip, and hundreds of condos, along with manmade islands with shops on them. It was ridiculous for this tiny little island. They were planning to accommodate 5,000 visitors—four times the total population of Bimini. I went to see the guy. 'You don't have to do this,' I said. 'You could make money by using the phenomenal beauty of this place.' He wouldn't listen. So I told him I would have to oppose him. I was on the Bahamas National Trust at the time, and I said to the trust, 'We have to fight this thing.'"

The battle for Bimini's mangroves has flared and subsided like a persistent scrub fire ever since, in part reflecting the sympathies of the governing political party, whether pro-business or pro-environment. This tussle between real estate and the natural estate is the main reason I am here. (The sharks are a bonus.) If aquaculture has been the prime driver of mangrove decline in poorer countries, property development has been the villain in rich nations and their offshore playgrounds. Bimini's struggle is just the latest iteration of a global problem.

Thanks to the efforts of Gruber and others, though, a small victory was won in December 2008 when the whole of East Bimini, which is predominantly mangroves, was declared a marine reserve, along with adjacent seagrass flats, sand banks, and coastal waters. Part of the protected area had been slated for the new Bimini Bay Resort's golf course. A well-struck tee shot would have landed in almost the same spot where Martin Luther King penned his final speech. The boundaries of the reserve are not yet fixed in legislative concrete, nor have the rules and enforcement structure been put in place, but Gruber is hopeful that East Bimini's mangroves may have escaped the fate of being turned into fairways and greens, the nurseries of the sea traded for vacationers' amusement.

It's not as if the nursery function of mangroves is some new discovery known only to cognoscenti. Rather, like most marine processes, it operates largely out of sight, and is easily underestimated or ignored. Biminites themselves have differing loyalties toward the islands' mangroves. Those whose livelihoods are most connected to the sea have a high regard for the linkages between commercially important species, such as Nassau grouper, bonefish, conch, and crawfish, and healthy mangrove stands and seagrass beds. "We don't even know what all kind of fish spawn here and go right out on the tide," Ansil Saunders told me. "Conch [larvae] float out north, south, east, west as far as twenty miles away."

"Bonefish Ebbie" David, another angling guide, lamented the loss of habitat, saying: "Everybody chewin' into mangroves. Sooner or later we won't have a fishin' village no more."

Bonefishing guides such as Saunders and David find themselves in a cleft stick. Tourism developments are good for their business, but if the environment is compromised, they won't have a business. Biminites who are less immediately reliant on the sea have fewer qualms about the loss of a little mangrove habitat. For some, progress comes from the blade of a bulldozer.

That reality manifests itself one morning when Matt Potenski, a whale-shark researcher and underwater photographer, takes me for a snorkel dive in mangroves near the lab. We slip into the lagoon and swim toward the fringing mangroves. The prop roots form cloisters and grottoes through which fish glide like birds through a woodland. It is easy to see how effectively mangroves perform their role as a sanctuary: fish simply melt into the forest.

The roots themselves have thick growths of fire sponge and other filter-feeders on them. Clusters of sharp-shelled mangrove oysters gleam like white coins on the trunks. On the seagrass beds beside the mangroves are hundreds of upside-down jellyfish, a type of jellyfish that appears to wish it were a sea anemone, because it lies on its "back" (the bell) with its frilly tentacles pointing upward. In this jellyfish garden the seabed has been turned into volcanoes of sand, each mound about the diameter of a football. These mini-Vesuviuses are the excavations of a tubeworm that burrows deep into the substrate. Bryan Franks told me that if you're really quick with a shovel you can dig up the worm, though usually it retreats to the bottom of its tunnel faster than a person can dig.

We snorkel along the edge of a channel into a large, oval embayment called the Duck Pond, and look up with surprise. An excavator and a front-end loader are being used to build a causeway. They are about three-quarters of the way across the pond. Potenski is dismayed. The causeway will almost certainly disrupt tidal circulation to a swathe of mangroves—a death sentence. This sheltered backwater is known to be an important shark habitat. The reclamation could end that. Despite the decade-long battle to defend Bimini's mangroves, here, almost within earshot of the lab, a local businessman is playing fast and loose with a few more.

The outgoing tide is picking up speed and carrying a plume of sediment from the earthworks out into the lagoon. Where we were following fish through the mangrove labyrinth thirty minutes earlier, now we can't see a thing. The consequences of such heavy sediment displacement can be dire. A Shark Lab study found that the first-year survival rate of newborn lemon sharks decreased 30 percent in nursery areas affected by the spoils of dredging and reclamation in North Bimini.

In the afternoon we take a boat trip through the tidal creeks and mangrove stands of East Bimini, the area to be protected by the new marine reserve. We pass a smart motor launch on the outer coast, but in the mangrove channels we are the only visitors. From the bow of the skiff we see spotted rays, jacks, and conch. A green turtle speeds away from us, launching itself out of the water and then splashing down and diving into the shadows. The day is so hot it's a relief to snorkel again. I squeeze myself into the mangrove-root matrix, wishing I could shrink down to fish size and fly through this underwater forest. Under a ledge I find a nest of sheltering crawfish and watch a three-foot barracuda cruise the turtlegrass flats. Ozymandias fish, I call them, because their jutting jaw reminds me of the "sneer of cold command" of Shelley's poem.

At dusk we idle past the manmade islands, marinas, and condos of Bimini Bay Resort. On board is former Shark Lab manager Grant Johnson, who has been in the front line of protest against the resort. For him, it is not just the destructive impact on habitat that is offensive. There is also an element of environmental racism. "The developer wants to turn Bimini into Florida's playground," he says. "The attitude is, if the land's not high enough, make it higher; if there's water where we want land to be, reclaim it; if there's land where we want water to be, dredge it. But people live here. This is their home we're talking about, not a desert island."

We pass a dike meant to confine sediment from an area of current construction. The high tide is lapping over the top, rendering the barrier useless. Johnson shakes his head, as if to say, "Can't these guys do anything right?" Bimini is far from the Bahamas' administrative center, in Nassau, and there is a frontier-style expediency to the place—the very spirit that attracted Hemingway in the 1930s. Johnson would like Bimini to be known as a frontier of nature, where people can see the sharks, swim with the dolphins, and kayak through the unspoiled mangroves. The upscale behemoth we're passing, still only in the first of three phases of construction, makes that dream a tenuous one.

Perhaps because it is just a speck in the ocean, Bimini focuses the mind on a seemingly intractable problem: choosing between competing demands for a finite resource. One man looks at Bimini's mangrove expanse and sees condos and a golf course. Another sees an ecotourism opportunity. Another sees a site for scientific research. Which vision should prevail? Do the spoils go to the highest bidder? The most persuasive lobbyist? Should the issue be decided by majority vote? Or by assessing the greatest good for the greatest number?

The crux of the issue is undoubtedly valuation, but the difficulty is that some values are highly tangible while others are not. It is self-evident that resorts deliver jobs and income (though perhaps not in the quantities that developers effusively promise). But you wouldn't necessarily know that healthy mangroves are nurseries for sharks and refuges for fish and lobsters, or that they have a long history as storm shelters, that they undergird the health of coral reefs, or even that they provided inspiration and solace for America's greatest civil rights leader in his darkest hour. Put those intangible values together—along with many others, which I will explore in the final chapter—and the one-time sacrifice of a forest ecosystem for a tourist playground looks like a far less valid option. Indeed, lopping down mangroves could be considered as wanton an act as shooting your initials into the head of a tiger shark.

The evidence from Bimini suggests that mangroves and the land on which they stand won't be saved until a correct scale of values is established, and public ambivalence about these saltwater thickets turns into respect for them as a vital natural resource. I see that Johnson has the word "hope" tattooed on his arm. He's going to need it. We all are, if we are to preserve the ecological and cultural wealth of the rainforests of the sea.

Seu Manuel (left) has spent most of his life catching mangrove mud crabs on the north-eastern coast of Brazil. The livelihood of crab catchers is increasingly threatened by the expansion of shrimp aquaculture (below) at the expense of mangrove forests. In the village of Curral Velho, Alouiso Rodrigues dos Santos (bottom) laments the loss of his fertile land, turned into a salt marsh by brine leaking from a shrimp farm on his boundary.

The battle for Bimini's mangroves has pitted the expansionist vision of Bimini Bay Resort (below) against the conservation ethos of Bimini Biological Field Station, where volunteers such as Hollie Neibert (right) conduct an annual census of lemon sharks, which use Bimini's mangroves as a nursery. Boat-builder Ansil Saunders (bottom) twice took Martin Luther King Jr. into the Bimini mangroves when the civil rights leader needed a place for quiet contemplation.

Tanzania's *Rufiji Delta* holds the largest expanse of mangroves in eastern Africa. The waterways that thread through the forests are the main travel routes for the people of the delta (left), and the trees provide poles for houses (bottom) and lumber for the building of traditional dhow (below). As elsewhere in the developing world, the specter of shrimp farming hangs over the delta's mangroves.

The harvesting of golpata, the mangrove palm (below), and wild mangrove honey (right) are just two of the livelihoods carried out in the Bangladesh Sundarbans. An armada of fishers (bottom) use fine nets to sieve the region's rivers for shrimp fry to supply a growing shrimp-farming industry.

In Panama, Candy Feller (left), studies the ecology of Pelliciera rhizophorae, *a New World mangrove with a showy, star-shaped flower. Rosabel Miró, director of the Panama Audubon Society (bottom), visits the residents of Juan Díaz, on the outskirts of Panama City, who eke out a subsistence life in the mangroves. In Chame, the making of mangrove charcoal (below) is a time-honored tradition.*

Jin Eong Ong (top) has made a lifetime study of carbon pathways in the mangrove forests of Malaysia—much of it atop a 65-foot tower. Robin Lewis (right) has fine-tuned methods of mangrove restoration in several Florida wetlands, such as West Lake Park, near Fort Lauderdale. In Picayune Strand State Forest, Andy From, of the US Geological Survey, and his colleagues (above) ponder the best route to reach sampling stations where he is monitoring changes in the area's hydrology.

Gordon Sato, an octogenarian cell biologist and humanitarian (bottom), has masterminded the planting of mangroves on the drought-stricken Eritrean coastline to provide a fodder source for livestock. Women from the village of Hirgigo harvest propagules from flourishing five-year-old mangrove trees (left), which they use to both plant new areas of coastline (below) and feed their sheep and goats.

Ecuador is home to some of the tallest
mangroves in the world. At El Majagual
(bottom) Elaine Corets, of the Mangrove
Action Project, is introduced to a giant
bromeliad-studded Rhizophora mangrove.
Despite massive mangrove loss in the past fifty
years, reserves in the north of the country
sustain traditional harvesting of mangrove
cockles by conchera such as Aracely Caicedo
(right), while in the south conservation-
minded fishers (below) plant mangrove
propagules in areas cleared for shrimp farms.

Chapter 8

Candy and the Magic Forest

In a few hours we sail round Cape Finisterre. I shall collect
plants and fossils and make astronomic observations. But that's
not the main purpose of my expedition—I shall try to find out
how the forces of nature interact upon one another and how
the geographic environment influences plant and animal life.
In other words, I must find out about the unity of nature.
—ALEXANDER VON HUMBOLDT, *Personal Narrative of a*
Journey to the Equinoctial Regions of the New Continent

O N T H E I S L A N D S of the Belize Barrier Reef, the roots of the
red mangrove dip like long fingers into the sea. They are so
thickly encrusted with marine organisms that they are like living paintings—Kandinsky canvases of vibrant color and form. Ver-
million, gray, and brick-orange sponges compete so fiercely for space
that they form long, luxuriant living icicles that drip off the sides.
Where mauve and jet-black sea squirts have gained a footing, they jut
out like jewels. Feather-duster tubeworms display their fragile plumes,
withdrawing them in a flash into gnarled brown tubes if disturbed.
Currents ripple the coronas of sea anemones—parchment-white

tentacles with baby-pink tips. Shoals of baby squid perform comical synchronized swimming routines. A sea urchin in a mangrove-root alcove twitches its long black spines. Strangest of all, to my eye, is a rust-colored arrow crab that looks like an underwater daddy longlegs with a pair of dainty blue pincers at the end of each claw.

The whole underwater forest seems alive, dancing with the wave movement. The roots, which reach down meters into the water, jiggle as if tapping to a beat that human ears can't hear. I rise to the surface and let the water line split my field of vision in two. This is the perfect viewpoint for a mangrove: half and half, a foot in each world. Above me, tree crabs prowling through the leaves. Below me, fish shoaling through the roots.

Nearby, snorkeling fully clothed as if she had just fallen out of the boat, is Candy Feller. She lies motionless, lost in the underwater pageant. Entranced still—though she has been studying these mangroves for twenty-five years.

Candy came to mangroves through art. She was a scientific illustrator, drawing beetles for the Smithsonian Institution. The Smithsonian needed someone to illustrate the marine organisms growing on mangrove roots in Belize. But there was a catch: the drawings had to be done in situ, under water. Candy could dive, so she got the job. She strapped on her scuba gear, took pencils and sheets of acetate, and became an underwater Audubon, sketching the life that encrusts every square inch.

Mangroves captivated her. They reminded her of the rhododendron and mountain laurel thickets she played in as a child in North Carolina—the feeling of being enclosed and embraced by nature. One of the scientists in Belize told her that very little was known about the insects that live in the mangrove canopy—that there was a world there waiting to be discovered, if she cared to take on the challenge. She did. She put away her Rotring pens and paintbrushes and went back to school to study. "I thought, 'I can tackle this,'" she said. "All these wonderful creepy-crawly critters that nobody knows about. It was like venturing into the unknown."

Candy has been shining a light into that unknown ever since. I have sought her out because she has become a specialist in something called biocomplexity—the way living systems interconnect with their physical environment, each shaping the other. She is going to unpack for me some of the intricacies of mangrove ecosystems—a world of interactions that, if only they were more widely known, would surely give pause to those who pass a death sentence on these apparently worthless wetlands.

The Smithsonian field station in Belize is on a pocket-handkerchief atoll called Carrie Bow Cay, one of a thousand palm-studded islands scattered along the Meso-American Barrier Reef. A short boat-hop away from Carrie Bow is Candy's main research site, Twin Cays (which, when Candy says it, sounds like "Twinkies"). From the air the twinned islands look like nestled yin and yang figures, with a channel running between them. I had joined Candy on one of her regular engagements with LightHawk, a nonprofit organization made up of volunteer pilots who donate their time and aircraft for environmental causes. Candy uses LightHawk to document the changes in mangrove cover in the countries where she is working. Those changes are usually negative, and usually manmade. Coming down the coast from Belize City, we flew over several massive shrimp farms carved out of the mangrove fringe. Some of the ponds were the size of fifteen football fields. Aerators stirred the water, leaving white cappuccino streaks of froth on the surface. Other stretches of coast bore the scars of commercial subdivision and resort construction. The two pincers of development—aquaculture and real estate—are squeezing mangroves out of the Belizean landscape, as they are throughout the Americas.

As we circled Twin Cays, Candy noticed a fresh scar of cut mangroves stretching along the shore. It was a survey line, she said—another local developer fixing to get a slice of the tourism pie. Mangroves are legally protected in Belize, but the cutting continues. "Developers have the attitude that they don't need a permit," says Candy. "They have money, and there are pliant politicians who will turn a blind eye. It's enough to make a person really mad." Half a dozen houses have been built on Twin Cays since 1980, when Smithsonian scientists first started visiting the islands as part of a long-term study of the reef-seagrass-mangrove complex. Candy's nightmare is to find one day that Twin Cays has become a resort, its mangroves relegated to a few ornamental clumps, and thirty years of study abruptly terminated.

Later we follow the survey line on foot, photographing the machete-slashed roots. A few students from the lab have joined us for an impromptu lesson in mangrove ecology—and mangrove threats. Candy pushes through the taller fringing red mangroves into a forest of dwarves. She wrote her PhD dissertation about these trees, which she calls her Charlie Brown mangroves. Though only the size of shrubs, they have all the attributes of adult trees. Dozens of stilt roots spring from their trunks, arching out and sinking into the waterlogged soil. Candy points to the pattern of leaf scars on their branches. Each time a leaf falls, a permanent record of its existence is left on the branch. Between two and three leaves fall off per year, so the number of leaf scars gives an estimate of the age of the tree. (You can't use the normal method of counting rings because mangroves do not lay down rings annually, but on a more erratic basis.) Though these dwarf trees are only a meter tall, they are several hundred years old.

What has limited their growth? This was the question Candy addressed in her PhD research. She found that one of the causes was lack of phosphorus. Mangroves at the edge of the island, with their roots dangling in the tide, get enough phosphorus from the seawater. The inland mangroves, with less frequent tidal flushing, are phosphorus-limited. When she provided phosphate fertilizer, the dwarf trees put on a flush of new growth.

The study has spurred a new line of research into the role of nutrients in mangrove ecosystems. Driving it is concern over the mounting avalanche of nutrients flowing from the land into the sea. Nutrient overenrichment poses a major threat to shallow-water ecosystems such as seagrass beds and coral reefs, which are geared to low nutrient levels. "If you add nutrients to a coral reef, you get an algal reef," says Candy.

Mangroves are effective at soaking up nutrient runoff from the land. This is one of their ecological services to the environment— a service that deforestation progressively eliminates. But long-term fertilization experiments conducted by Candy and her colleagues in Belize, Panama, Florida, and elsewhere have shown that mangroves, too, are susceptible to overenrichment; in fact, it can kill them.

It turns out we're destroying mangroves not only by cutting them down but also—ironically—by artificially boosting their growth. Allowing nutrients, especially nitrogen, to disperse unchecked into mangroves promotes the growth of above-ground structures such as leaves and stems, but not of roots. The trees look green and lush, but their canopy is writing checks their root system can't cash. Like any plants living in a desert (in the mangroves' case, an osmotic "desert" of saline soil), survival depends on balancing the water lost through leaf transpiration with the water taken up by the roots. Despite the harsh conditions they endure, mangroves are very good at maintaining this balance. Their water-use efficiency is among the highest of any terrestrial ecosystem. But the extra growth put on as a result of increased nitrogen uptake forces the trees into physiological overdraft. Their roots can't keep up with demand. It takes only a small reduction in rainfall (a water "recession," to extend the financial metaphor) to cause the trees' internal water economy to crash.

The ramifications are broad. The idea that mangroves will magically mitigate poor farming practice or wasteful nutrient management on land turns out to be flawed. And the idea that coastlines can be artificially greened and turned into coastal buffers by fast-tracking mangrove growth through massive fertilizer applications is also faulty. Yes, nutrient enrichment causes mangroves to flourish during favorable periods, but it may set up the forests for a crash during times of water stress. There's another downside. Fostering leaf and branch growth at the expense of the roots increases the likelihood that the trees will become top-heavy and sustain damage—or be toppled—during storms and tsunamis. Their ability to function as coastal shields is compromised.

We walk on through the Lilliputian mangroves, sometimes sinking to our knees in the slushy sediment. It's like walking through thick soup. The soil here is the finest peat, formed from billions of roots composting over thousands of years. Candy says the peat is two meters (seven feet) thick—most of it from fine mangrove roots. It accumulates so quickly that mangrove islands such as Twin Cays are rising by a few millimeters a year.

Several saltwater ponds dot the interior of the islands. They are full of upside-down jellyfish and a delicate alga with surely the most beautiful name of any seaweed: mermaid's wineglass. The "wineglasses" are clusters of fluted green or white cups, about an inch in diameter, borne on long, slender stalks. Nosing around them in the shallow water are chubby fish called checkered puffers.

Candy starts poking among the branches of her bonsai trees, looking for critters. During the course of her research she has found more than a hundred species of arthropod (insects, spiders, crustaceans, and their ilk) associated with the twigs of red mangrove. Included in this pantheon are termites, scorpions, puss moths, roaches, bag worms, mites, spiders, and many more. Thirty-five of them are wood-feeders, and seven are specialist wood-boring beetle and moth larvae that feed exclusively on *Rhizophora mangle* twigs.

Wood borers function as "ecosystem engineers"—gamechangers whose activities alter the ecological playing field for other creatures. A wood borer, for instance, may drill out the core of a living twig, killing it. When the borer leaves, its exit hole becomes an entranceway for the next species in the chain—perhaps a borer that feeds only on dead wood. Still later, the hollowed-out twig may be occupied by ants, crickets, or even, as Candy discovered, a species of carnivorous ribbon worm that feeds by everting its gut, wrapping it around the prey and swallowing it whole.

Candy has more than just a zoological interest in these creatures. She wants to learn how the nutrient overenrichment of mangroves affects herbivores and upper trophic levels in the food web. "Nutrients are the currency of food webs," she says. She adds nutrients to experimental plots, then follows how they move through the ecosystem in the same way an auditor follows a money trail. The three major elements she's interested in (the dollars and cents) are carbon, nitrogen, and phosphorus. She compares the ratios of each element in the mangrove trees in her study plots, and also in the herbivores that eat mangroves.

Candy believes that herbivores have a far greater influence on the structure and function of mangrove ecosystems than they are usually credited with. "They control both the amount and the distribution of forest biomass," she says. A sprouting mangrove propagule, for instance, may have terrestrial borers burrowing down from the top and marine borers burrowing up from the bottom. From her studies, Candy estimates that as many as 99 percent of red-mangrove propagules are killed by wood borers.

A somewhat larger sphere of influence is held by a type of beetle larva that girdles entire mangrove branches, cutting off the sap flow. When the dead branch eventually crashes to the sediment, it creates a light gap in which formerly shaded seedlings can flourish. Still another group with an outsize influence are leaf-rolling psyllids. Leaf rolling in *Avicennia germinans,* the New World black mangrove, has been found to reduce leaf area (and thus photosynthetic productivity) by 40 percent. To think: a louse the size of a sesame seed controls the energy flow to an entire community.

Candy hollers. She has found one of her favorite insects, a golden wood-boring cerambycid (longhorn beetle) larva, which spends ten years building galleries in mangrove timber. The larva faces an interesting life-history conundrum. If it pupates in the safety of its enclosed internal gallery, how will it get out once it has metamorphosed into an adult? The adult lacks wood-chewing mouthparts. Imagine it. It would be like waking up in a coffin. Without a drill.

There is an elegant solution: the larva creates an exit hole for the adult. So now the adult can get out, but what is to stop a predator getting in? Another problem, another solution. As the grub chews through the bark to the outside, the tree responds by producing a gummy exudate. The larva uses the gum to seal the exit. The gum hardens into a temporary cap, protecting the vulnerable pupa within. After a period of weeks or months, rain dissolves the gum, releasing the metamorphosed beetle from its sarcophagus.

We move to higher ground, where we find *Rhizophora mangle*'s usual companions, making up the New World trio of mangrove species: *Laguncularia racemosa*, with short, gnarled pneumatophores, like arthritic fingers, and *Avicennia germinans*, with such a dense spread of aerial roots that it looks as if someone has sown a crop of pencils. It has been estimated that an *Avicennia* measuring three meters (10 feet) tall may have more than 10,000 pneumatophores in its ventilation system. *Avicennia*'s aerators are never taller than about a foot, whereas a species of *Sonneratia* in Asia produces enormous root spikes that are taller than a human being.

I ask Candy if she thinks there is any truth to the claim that *Rhizophora* roots are such efficient water purifiers that thirsty soldiers fighting in the Pacific during World War II stripped off the bark and sucked fresh water from the internal root tissue. "Let's try it," she says, producing a penknife. She peels a couple of small roots back to the pith and we try the soldiers' trick, but no amount of sucking can extract even a drop.

The principle is correct, though. Mangroves in the *Rhizophora* genus use an ultrafiltration mechanism to restrict salt from entering their roots, with the result that *Rhizophora* sap is less than 1/100th the salinity of the substrate. Theirs is one of two main strategies that mangroves have for regulating salt in their tissues. The other, championed by *Avicennia*, among others, is to partially block salt at the roots and get rid of the excess through salt glands in the leaves. So while red mangroves are salt excluders, black mangroves are both excluders and exuders. Salt management is physiologically costly to a plant—it takes energy to oppose the osmotic inflow of salt and outflow of water. The reason mangroves are restricted to warm latitudes may be that only some kind of super-mangrove could deal with the demands of both salt and cold.

We scan the branches for boa constrictors and the spiny-tailed iguanas that locals call "wish willies." The iguanas elude us, but we find a boa zigzagged along a dead branch, all fawn and brown dapples and gleaming scales, taking its ease in the shade.

On our way back through the dwarf mangroves, I try to comprehend the fact that this is an old-growth forest. If these trees were as tall as those of El Majagual, they would be considered a national treasure. Because they are dwarves, they are considered bulldozer fodder. In the Bahamas, the Bimini Bay Resort development company justified the destruction of similar stands of "stunted mangroves" on the grounds that the trees were biological runts—losers in the game of life. Yet who can say how many creatures owe their existence to such trees?

As much as Candy loves her bonsai mangroves in Belize, there are forests in Panama that she adores still more—magical places where the mangroves drip with epiphytes, where shimmering blue butterflies float through the forest and hummingbirds feed on the nectar of the mangrove blossoms. At the height of the flowering season, the air is full of the squeaking of hummingbirds. "Imagine being strafed by hummingbirds," Candy said when I first met her. Right then the seed of a Panama trip was planted.

Four years later I am traveling with Candy, two of her field assistants, and a visiting ornithologist through the mangrove-topped islets of Bocas del Toro, the "mouths of the bull," an archipelago on Panama's Caribbean coast near the border with Costa Rica. Candy has several research sites here, where she is conducting mangrove nutrient experiments like those in Belize.

We travel by speedboat. The sea is silky smooth and dotted with the canoes of the Ngöbe Buglé people native to this area. They are fishing, diving, or just commuting; rivers and sea are the only roads in this area.

At Peninsula Valiente we stop at a village of rough timber buildings on stilts at the water's edge, blue smoke drifting through almond trees, jungle rising thickly behind. Half an hour farther on we come to Candy's magic forest, a grove of *Pelliciera rhizophorae,* a New World mangrove that was thought to be extinct on the Caribbean coast and to survive on the Pacific coast only patchily, from Costa Rica to northern Ecuador. Here on the shores of Panama's Chiriqui Lagoon, Candy has discovered *Pelliciera* stands with more than eight million trees.

Pelliciera trees have fluted buttress roots, straight trunks, and clusters of long, elliptical leaves. But it is their flowers that set them apart. Almost all mangroves have small, unspectacular flowers; *Pelliciera* produces showy, star-shaped, nectar-filled blooms. The nectar attracts hummingbirds (believed to be the tree's main pollinator) as well as many insects. Even tree crabs take a wee dram.

On a previous trip, Candy discovered something unusual: when she shone a UV light on the flowers, the nectar fluoresced. Today she wants to take nectar samples and have them analyzed in the United States by a lab that specializes in fluorescence. Collecting nectar turns out to be too easy. The flowers produce so much nectar that she can fill a glass capillary tube in seconds—if she beats me to it. I've been in a sugar desert lately, and am making up for it by licking *Pelliciera* nectar. It has a delicate caramel flavor. I start imagining *Pelliciera* crème brûlée. Give me a thousand *Pelliciera* blooms and a thousand capillary tubes. . . .

We hear a loud whirring and look up to see a flash of magenta wings as a hummingbird sips from a flower. The hummers aren't exactly in strafing numbers—this isn't the peak of the season—but watching their darting, beelike visits from bloom to bloom is wonderful.

I walk through the forest, scouting for flowers and hummingbirds and watching for the peacock flash of blue morpho butterflies, whose seemingly random fluttering is somehow always out of camera range. For a while, the best I can achieve photographically is a morpho at rest on a mangrove leaf. The wings are folded, concealing the heavenly blue, but the outside of the wings is sumptuous in its own way: charcoal gray, with a set of false eyes picked out in black, white, and yellow. Then I find a morpho trapped in a golden orb weaver's web, with the spider feeding on its dead body. The weaver is an impressive creature in itself. Herself, I should say—the males are inconsequentially small. Female golden orb weavers reach about four centimeters (two inches) in body length, with banded burgundy-and-orange legs that have tufts of bristles that look like small black bottlebrushes. This web is about three feet across. It is the silk that is golden, not the weaver, and, indeed, the strands look like spun bullion. The American Museum of Natural History is said to have in its collection a piece of cloth woven from the silk of a million golden orb weavers. They are truly the Rumpelstiltskin of arachnids.

In from the tall edge forest is an area of dwarf *Pelliciera*. Here, as in Belize, the soils are oligotrophic—nutrient-limited. Phosphorus is the limiting element in the dwarf forest, while nitrogen limits the growth of the shoreline fringe. Candy and her coworkers fan out to collect seedlings, twigs, flowers, crabs, and winkles. I help with the fiddler crabs, known in Spanish as the *cangrejo violinista*. I catch tree crabs, too, riffling my fingers through the tufting liverworts on the trunks of the *Pelliciera,* where small *Aratus* like to hide. All of the plant and animal samples will be taken back to the lab for chemical analysis, to see how Candy's fertilizer treatments are filtering through the food web.

I push through the dwarf forest to the back of the stand, where the stilt roots of huge old *Rhizophora* leapfrog across the mud. Some of the roots extend 10 meters (33 feet) or more from the trunk, looping and relooping, touching down on the mud and then branching out again. I am by no means the first to think of red mangroves as "walking trees." Aborigines in northern Australia believe that a species of *Rhizophora* is the embodiment of a primal ancestor, Giyapara, who walked across the mudflats and created the coastal plains.

Negotiating the tanglewood of roots in a mature *Rhizophora* forest is a challenge that has vexed anyone setting foot in these places. An Australian mangrove biologist is said to hold the world record for the 100-yard dash through a mangrove swamp: twenty-two minutes and thirty seconds!

David Luther, an ornithologist who works on the conservation of endangered bird species at the University of Maryland, is clambering among the *Rhizophora* roots, too. He carries a heavy tape recorder, which he uses not just to record but to play the calls of species he glimpses in the canopy. When a bird hears the call of its own kind, curiosity or territorial aggression will often compel it to investigate.

Luther has just published a list of terrestrial vertebrates that depend on mangroves for their survival—mangrove endemics, as they are known. The list includes forty-eight birds, fourteen reptiles, one amphibian, and six mammals. Among them are a terrapin, two monitors, several snakes (including such taxonomic mouthfuls as the red-tailed green rat snake and the dog-faced water snake), a number of rails, kingfishers, hummingbirds, flycatchers, whistlers, sunbirds and honeyeaters, and, among the mammals, the proboscis monkey of Borneo, two Cuban hutias (like giant guinea pigs), two bats, and the pygmy three-toed sloth, the latter found only on a single island in Bocas del Toro.

Luther believes that such species have become mangrove specialists either through being outcompeted in adjacent inland habitats or through being forced to use the mangroves as refuges during extreme climate events. He speculates, for instance, that during the arid millennia of the Pleistocene, when wet forests contracted and disappeared in continents such as Australia, some species entered the mangroves as a last resort. Once there, they began to specialize on food sources such as crabs and certain types of nectar. At least a third of the species on Luther's list now feed primarily on food sources not available in adjacent terrestrial habitats.

One of Luther's mangrove endemics is trilling in the branches above our heads as we talk: the mangrove yellow warbler, a sparrow-sized bird with canary-colored plumage. The male has a rusty red head, as if it had been dipped in paprika. In Spanish it is called *reinita manglera*, princess of the mangroves. As a species, the little princess remains widespread, but almost half of the mangrove endemics are endangered, many of them critically so. By restricting themselves to mangroves, they have hitched their wagon to a fading star. Like island endemics, whose safe oases become death traps when alien predators are introduced, species restricted to mangroves have nowhere to escape to when their habitat is destroyed.

Luther and I return to the shore to eat a lunch of boiled eggs, tomatoes, bread, and sugar-sweet pineapples bought from Indians in a passing canoe. Someone shouts and points, and I am in time to see a plumed basilisk running across the river and up a mangrove tree. In Greek mythology, a basilisk was the king of serpents. Part rooster, part snake and part lion, it could slay a person with a single glance. Our endearing little lizard, shamrock-green from head to tail, with a sail-like crest along its back and large golden eyes, seems an unlikely smiter—more suited to its other name, the Jesus Christ lizard, acquired because of its ability to walk on water.

As the tide rises, I sink a few plastic tumblers into the mud to see if I can catch an unusual fish called the mangrove rivulus. After an hour the cups are full of water, but no rivulus have entered. Candy has better luck. She finds several of the slender, inch-long fishes swimming in shallow puddles among the *Pelliciera* trunks, darting down fiddler crab burrows when disturbed. Their claim to fame is that they are the only known vertebrate capable of breeding without a mate. They have bifunctional gonads, producing both eggs and sperm, and fertilize their own eggs internally.

As well as being able to clone themselves, they can breathe air through their skin, like a frog, and one specimen was observed to spend sixty-six consecutive days out of water, living in a hole in a tree. Their ability to survive out of water comes in handy for rivulus researchers: they exchange live specimens through the post. Scientists speculate that the fish's hermaphroditic style of reproduction may have evolved in response to their extremely isolated existence. Being holed up for long periods in a dry crab burrow does not allow rivulus much of a social life.

The specimen-of-the-day award, however, goes not to the lizard that walks on water or the fish that lives in air but to an extraordinary caterpillar that Candy finds on the trunk of a *Pelliciera*. As long and thick as a finger, it has a snake-shaped head and a single Cyclops eye in the middle of its abdomen, complete with a fake eyelid that blinks. Its skin has dazzling geometric patterns in chocolate brown and moss green. To complete the snake mimicry, the caterpillar raises its head if you breathe on it, as if to strike.

The creature is positioned head down, perhaps so that a predatory bird will mistakenly target the decoy eye or be frightened away by it. The trunk is bare of liverworts around the caterpillar, and looks to have been grazed by it. None of us has seen a caterpillar like it. Later, when I send photographs to Annette Aiello, a Smithsonian entomologist, she says that it is a new species to her, too, and that it probably belongs to the family of sphinx moths, which includes several snake mimics.

Sated with observation and loaded with specimens, we start the journey back to the lab, but Candy can't resist exploring a new river system on the way. The river is lined with *Pelliciera*. Their buttress roots and the reflections they cast produce a row of diamond shapes at the waterline. Some of the trees are flowering, and a few have propagules hanging from them. They look like flattened lemon squeezers. When they fall to the forest floor they open like castanets, allowing the seedling to spring up.

The trees are festooned with epiphytes. Bromeliads, orchids, and arum lilies perch and twine on trunks that are felted with moss, liverwort, and filmy fern. Candy thinks of the epiphyte community as a separate freshwater ecosystem suspended over the saltwater mangrove one and sustained by the generous humidity and rainfall of the area. The epiphytes and their associated fauna add an additional level of intricacy to the system—another stratum in the three-dimensional chess game of this forest's ecology.

Candy stands in the bow of the boat, surveying the forest, drinking in the detail, wondering out loud why the *Pelliciera* on this coast seem to reach a certain height and then stop growing, while they reach much greater heights on the Pacific coast. The birders in the group have eyes only for the trogons, toucans, and other avian exotica we see, but Candy is glued to the mangroves, pondering the delicious complexity her work is helping define.

Chapter 9

The Carbon Sleuth

It's red mangrove trees versus greenhouse gases
at the Super Bowl in Miami Sunday.
—*Reuters news agency, January 30, 2007*

OR THE PAST FEW YEARS, when the United States' top
football teams take to the field for the championship final
on Super Bowl Sunday, two goals have already been scored
before the game starts—for mangroves and for climate. Since
2005, the National Football League has planted thousands of mangroves and other native trees to offset the carbon dioxide emitted
during the event. The NFL calculates that the trees it plants pick up
the tab for the 500 tonnes of carbon dioxide released into the atmosphere from electricity generation, vehicle use, and 100,000
cheering fans at the venue. Mangroves help make the Super Bowl
carbon neutral, claims the NFL.

It's not just professional sport that is greening up its act. Across
the industrial landscape, from airlines to agriculture, the idea of offsetting carbon emissions by planting forests is taking root. The ability of trees to capture atmospheric carbon dioxide and store it in
their woody tissues gives them a leading role as carbon sinks, absorbing and sequestering the rampant element that is resetting the
planetary thermostat.

Long before climate science became a hot ticket (so to speak), before carbon footprinting became as de rigueur as DNA fingerprinting, an amiable Malaysian professor with a fondness for durian was working his way toward an understanding of how carbon flows through a mangrove forest. "Closing the carbon budget" is how he describes his work: comparing carbon inputs and outputs and following the carbon trail. Some of the research took place atop a 20-meter (66-foot) tower in the Matang mangrove reserve in northwest Peninsular Malaysia, a plantation that has been logged on a thirty-year rotation for a century—the longest sustainably harvested mangrove forest in the world.

Ong Jin Eong is going to take me there. But first, there is the small matter of a durian to be consumed. Actually, it is large matter. Durians are the size of a football and can weigh up to three kilograms (seven pounds). Ong has bought one for me to try. It lies in thorny splendor in the fruit bowl at his home on Penang Island. He presents it to me for the sniff test. I'm expecting to have the gag reaction described by generations of travel writers, including Mark Twain, who reported that the stench was of "so atrocious a nature that when a durian was in the room even the presence of a polecat was a refreshment." In truth, it isn't so bad—though perhaps this is some kind of tourist durian, genetically modified so as not to offend the delicate foreign nose.

Ong slices through the armor-plated rind and we go to work on the custardy pulp that surrounds the seeds, sucking the sweet white flesh and spitting out the giant pips. Twain has useful advice on the process: "[Durian eaters] said that if you could hold your nose until the fruit was in your mouth a sacred joy would suffuse you from head to foot that would make you oblivious to the smell of the rind, but that if your grip slipped and you caught the smell of the rind before the fruit was in your mouth, you would faint."

My experience falls short of sacred joy but is higher than that of Anthony Burgess, who said consuming durians was "like eating sweet raspberry blancmange in the lavatory." I suspect you need to grow up with durians to become truly besotted with them.

Before we head south to Matang, Ong takes me to Merbok, on the mainland north of Penang. He wants to show me Malaysian mangroves at their most diverse. In Malaysia we are close to the center of mangrove biodiversity. Seventy million years ago, this region was part of the Tethys Sea, an oceanic rift between the supercontinents of Gondwana in the south and Laurasia in the north. Some scientists believe that mangroves originated here and gradually dispersed around the globe. According to this view, when Africa collided with Asia Minor 18 million years ago, cutting the world into two aquatic hemispheres, mangroves became separated into Old World and New World types. (Another theory holds that mangroves evolved independently in a number of locations.)

Today, Old World mangroves stretch from the Red Sea and East Africa to the central Pacific, with peak diversity occurring in Southeast Asia and northern Australia. New World mangroves—a totally separate group of species—occupy both sides of the Atlantic, the Caribbean, and the eastern Pacific, with a diversity spike in Panama and Colombia. These mangroves were themselves split into two groups when the Panama Gap closed three million years ago, isolating eastern Pacific mangroves from their Atlantic siblings.

Here in Merbok, Ong has identified fifty-seven species of mangroves and "mangrove associates"—species that are sometimes found in mangrove communities but that lack most or all of the adaptations of true mangroves, such as pneumatophores, stilt roots, and vivipary (the production of ready-to-grow propagules instead of dormant seeds). That tally, he says, places Merbok among the most species-diverse mangrove forests in the world.

We hire a boat at a smart new marina carved out of the mangroves and motor down the estuary. The forest rises from the ocher-colored waters like a glittering green wall. The main seaward trees are two species of *Rhizophora*, with trunks as straight as telegraph poles and prop roots as thick as whale ribs. Through the gaps we see big specimens of *Heritiera littoralis*, with planklike buttress roots to support their trunks; *Xylocarpus granatum*, with cannonball-sized propagules, known as the puzzle-nut mangrove because its triangular seeds are arranged so intricately inside the fruit as to resemble a wooden puzzle; four species of *Sonneratia*, called the mangrove apple because of its apple-shaped fruit. (Inside, they are nothing like an apple, being full of tiny seeds.) During the Japanese occupation of Malaysia in World War II, fishing communities are said to have eaten mangrove apples when other food was scarce—though Ong says the fruit tastes sour. In Sri Lanka, some mangrove communities have begun to use *Sonneratia* apples to make fruit juice, jam, chutney, and yogurt. In addition, they make corks from the bark and cultivate bonsai specimens for sale to tourists.

There is a curious ecological link between the mangrove apple and the durian. The flowers of some species of durian are pollinated by a nectar-sipping bat that feeds on *Sonneratia* flowers when durians are not in bloom. Clearance of mangroves is thought to have caused the bat population to decline, affecting durian pollination—to the alarm of durian devotees. One evening, Ong and I staked out a *Sonneratia* to see if we could catch a glimpse of a bat. The flowers open for only one night, so we had searched for a tree with buds that were beginning to burst. The flowers opened on cue, each a pompon of white stamens, but no bats showed up in our torch beams.

Sonneratia trees attract another nocturnal visitor: fireflies. In certain mangrove forests in the region, the night is lit by a galaxy of fireflies that flash in synchrony. It is the males that flash; females merely flicker and glow. The displays are probably connected to courtship, with some scientists suggesting that female fireflies choose the "flashiest" males. The flashing begins soon after sunset and persists through the night. It takes the fireflies on an individual tree about fifteen minutes to settle into a rhythm (usually half a second to a second between flashes), and any new arrivals quickly fall into step. Neighboring trees are often in sync, while more distant trees are not, so apparently there is a visual cue involved. Although individual fireflies live for only a few weeks, the display trees are more or less permanent fixtures. Malay fishermen use them for navigation—living lighthouses.

As we explore the arms of the Merbok estuary, now and then we see a brown patch in the cloak of green—tree skeletons with not a leaf on them. Ong thinks the most likely cause of death is beetle larvae boring into shoots in the canopy, disrupting the water-transport system and killing the tree.

Merbok's fishers are hard at work. At the side of a channel a woman with mud-flecked clothes and arms sits on the stern of a boat, kicking it along with her foot and pushing a shrimp net in front of her. The net is suspended between two bamboo poles with skids on their ends that run along the mud. She holds the handles as if plowing. But she's catching more trash than shrimp. Plastic bags, soda bottles, rags, and bits of polystyrene drift downstream from the town of Sungai Petani. The lower branches of the mangroves are littered with the stuff. The woman stops every few minutes to pick out the shrimp and flick the rubbish back into the water.

In another arm of the estuary a man fishing from a long-tail boat is doing better. The term "long tail" refers to the style of outboard motor, which looks like an ancient homemade weed trimmer with a very long shaft and a propeller at the end. The propeller spins just beneath the surface of the water, allowing the boats to navigate shallow mangrove channels. The fisherman says that on a good spring tide he can catch 50 kilograms (110 pounds) of shrimp in a haul. He leans over the side of his skiff, washing a colander-ful. He picks up a clump of shrimp to show me. They are small, about a centimeter in length, and the color of cooked white rice, with two black-pepper specks for eyes. This is the variety used to make shrimp paste, the ubiquitous base of Asian curries.

Near a settlement we see shellfish collectors walking through the mangroves, each trailing a machete in the mud, listening for the *ting* of metal hitting a mollusk shell. In the middle of the estuary we pass dozens of fish farms, each a cluster of pens and boardwalks with a wooden hut floating on blue plastic barrels. Behind a village restaurant where we stop for lunch, a family of fishers extract the gas bladders from a catch of fish. The membranous miniature balloons, also known as fish maw, are a luxury item in Asian cuisine, typically served deep-fried in soups.

It is as if the area had been parceled into designated harvest zones: shellfish here, shrimp nets here, push nets here, fish farming here. How long the harvest can be sustained is another matter. Merbok's mangroves are disappearing. "Each time I come here there is less and less," says Ong. Fifty years ago, the mangroves covered 80 square kilometers (31 square miles). Now they cover a quarter of that area. The rest has been cleared for rice and palm-oil plantations, shrimp ponds, and, more recently, housing estates.

Ong says that at the current rate of loss there will be no mangroves left in Merbok by 2020. Ironically, that is the year by which Malaysia is projected to have achieved developed-nation status. Economic growth and mangrove preservation remain mutually exclusive concepts in much of the developing world. This is because classical economics doesn't take into account non-market goods and services, says Ong, whose work on mangroves has helped establish the value of one such service: storing carbon—a service that is becoming critically important in a climate-stressed world.

On the drive to Matang, he tells me how disappointed he was that the Kyoto Protocol did not allow the inclusion of old-growth forests, including mangroves, in its cap-and-trade system. Signatories to Kyoto could not include such forests as assets in their carbon budgets, so there was no incentive from a carbon perspective to preserve them. The decision to omit existing forests from carbon-trading mechanisms was largely a political one, but at the time there was also a prevalent but erroneous view that old-growth forests are carbon neutral, with the input of carbon to the system from photosynthesis balanced by the output from respiration. Ong's work has shown that, on the contrary, old-growth mangroves are highly effective at taking carbon out of environmental circulation.

I climb with the sprightly, silver-haired professor to the top of the scaffolding tower where he and his team have made their measurements of photosynthesis, sap flow, respiration, and other biological processes in the leaves of the mangrove canopy. Over the quarter century that Ong has been auditing carbon in his mangrove patch, he has had to deal with an unusual hazard: the local macaques, which seem irresistibly drawn to the high-tech equipment. Staff would arrive in the morning to find data loggers knocked over, cables mangled, and sensors chewed. They resorted to putting plastic bags of shrimp paste next to the equipment in an attempt to redirect the monkeys' curiosity. "Monkeys have learned that plastic bags often contain goodies," Ong explains.

Monkey vandalism notwithstanding, Ong's group has been able to work out how much carbon is assimilated into mangrove leaves, how much is stored in living trees, and how much eventually makes its way into nearby waterways. The measurements suggest that the net productivity of a mangrove forest is as high as that of any natural ecosystem—about 150 kilograms of carbon per hectare (132 pounds per acre) per day—and that as much as a third of this organic production is eventually exported to coastal waters. Mangroves, it turns out, are fantastic carbon-processing plants, and their demolition robs the marine environment of a vital nutrient supply.

Ong's team has also shown that a significant portion of net carbon production in mangroves ends up in the forest sediment, remaining sequestered there for thousands of years. Anaerobic mangrove sediments act as molecular jails, locking up carbon by preventing its oxidation to climate-threatening carbon dioxide. Mangrove conversion, whether it be for shrimp ponds, agriculture, or real estate development, reverses the situation, changing a carbon sink into a carbon source and releasing the accumulated carbon back into the atmosphere—but fifty times faster than it was sequestered. This, says Ong, is a huge hidden cost of mangrove deforestation.

If mangroves were recognized as carbon-storage assets, that would radically alter the way these forests are valued, says Ong. In the new era of global emissions trading, in which forest-rich, carbon-absorbing countries sell offset credits to more industrialized, carbon-emitting countries, mangroves could win a stay of execution. But Ong notes that the financial incentives will have to be great enough to make forest preservation economically and politically viable.

"Take Indonesia, which has the largest total area of mangroves of any country in the world. It can't afford to save them for nothing," he says. "But if the Indonesians could trade the carbon-storage potential of their mangroves as a commodity, that would create a great incentive to stop bulldozing them for shrimp ponds or chipping them for the production of rayon."

For its part, Indonesia hasn't been rushing to embrace carbon-friendly policies. Despite making the right noises in international discussions about forest preservation, at the all-important local level permits to log and clear rainforests, including mangroves, are still being handed out. Indonesia loses 2.8 million hectares (7 million acres) of rainforest a year and recently overtook Malaysia as the world's largest producer of palm oil—an industry whose growth has come at the price of rainforest destruction. Moreover, Indonesia has been identified as the world's third-largest emitter of greenhouse gases, behind the United States and China, with three-quarters of its emissions arising from deforestation, peatland degradation, and forest fires. Yet if the right international pricing and policy mechanisms were put in place, there is no reason why even a carbon-spender like Indonesia could not become a saver.

In one Indonesian state at least—Aceh, where the 2004 Indian Ocean tsunami inflicted its greatest damage—moves are afoot to preserve old-growth forests through a new United Nations initiative called Reducing Emissions from Deforestation and Forest Degradation (REDD), which provides what Kyoto didn't: a mechanism to generate income from keeping existing trees standing—and sucking up carbon dioxide. At the 2009 Copenhagen climate talks, delegates gave a green light to the program, so there is now a good chance that "avoided deforestation"—the retention of existing forests, mangroves included—will be included in future global climate policy regimes.

Mangroves should feature high in REDD initiatives because they sequester up to fifty times more carbon in their soils than terrestrial tropical rainforests do. Meantime, there is no reason why countries that have already squandered their mangrove forest resources should not choose to replant, gaining both a tradable asset and a coastal defense—not to mention easing the planet's carbon burden.

Taiping, population about 200,000, is the nearest large town to Matang. I stroll the bustling streets, amused by store names such as the Rising Step Shoe Shop and the Hair Saloon (sadly, without swing doors) and intrigued by the miniature shrines tucked into alcoves on the sidewalk, each containing a few incense sticks, an offering of fruit and some cups of rice wine. Several large windowless buildings catch my eye. They look like bunkers with tiny slots in the walls for snipers. Ong tells me they are swiftlet nesting houses, for the production of nests for bird's-nest soup. We find a Chinese specialty store, and Ong asks the proprietor if he has any bird's nests. He reaches under the counter and produces an ornate box. Inside are a dozen compartments containing the pale gelatinous nests, which are made entirely from saliva by male swiftlets. Bird's nests are big business in Malaysia. There are reportedly 20,000 "swiftlet hotels" in the country. The owners play CDs of swiftlet calls to attract the birds to nest at their establishments. The most expensive nest variety, the red-blood nest—the Perigord truffle of bird's nests—can retail for up to $40,000 a kilogram.

Well to the other end of the commodity price spectrum is Matang charcoal, for which the manufacturers get a dollar a kilogram. Ong takes me to one of the charcoal works, where mangrove logs smolder inside igloo-shaped brick ovens. The 1.5-meter (5-foot) logs come in by boat. The timber is dense and heavy, each log 25 kilograms (55 pounds) or more. I heft one to my shoulder and imagine how fit I'd be if I lugged these around all day for a job.

Inside a hangarlike building half a dozen kilns stand in a line, each at a different stage of combustion. Workers load up to 40 tonnes of green wood into a kiln at the beginning of the month-long process. A fire is lit, and for the first ten days or so the kiln vents are left open to allow moisture to escape. When the wood is sufficiently dry (judged by the foreman's highly attuned sense of smell) the vents are blocked, the entrance is sealed with clay, and the conversion to charcoal begins. After ten days of cooking and a week of cooling, the kiln entrance is broken down and the carbonized logs, now a quarter of their original weight, are removed. In the factory I visited, women were doing most of the unloading. It was as hot as a sauna inside the kiln. Faces begrimed and clothes blackened, the women shuttled in and out, carrying the gray sticks, picking their way through the next load of logs.

Matang's 40,000 hectares (about 100,000 acres) of mangrove forest provide the raw material for between fifty and a hundred charcoal makers. The forest reserve was gazetted for the purpose of charcoal and timber production in 1906, and has been managed without loss of land to agriculture or aquaculture ever since. In fact, the forest area has increased by 1,500 hectares (3,700 acres) in the past century due to the accretion of sediment on the river deltas where it is situated. Mangroves colonize the new land, pushing the forest boundaries outward.

Matang is considered a model of sustainable mangrove forestry. There are very few plantation forests like it in the world. Three-quarters of the reserve is treated as productive forest, and the balance is protected. The timber yield per thirty-year rotation (not counting two bouts of thinning, the harvest from which is sold as poles) stands at about 170 tonnes per hectare (420 tons per acre).

When a section of forest, or coupe, is felled, it is immediately re-planted—a process that is not without its problems. The same macaques that give Ong grief on his tower cause foresters headaches by pulling up propagules after they have been planted, snapping them in half to get at the spongy edible tissue inside. Planting seedlings circumvents the monkey business, but is more time-consuming and costly than sticking propagules in the ground.

As a sideline to timber production, the forest is operated as an eco-tourism destination. A well-constructed boardwalk leads visitors through stands of *Rhizophora apiculata* that rise 15 meters (about 50 feet) sheer to the first branch and soar at least another 15 meters again to the top of the canopy. In gaps where enough sunlight penetrates, mangrove fern and sprouting *Rhizophora* and *Bruguiera* give a splash of green to the somber sediment. Some trees have ant nests on their dappled trunks, with covered walkways leading down to the soil.

At the seaward edge of the forest, fiddler crabs are feeding. Their mauve-tipped pincers are in constant motion, dipping into the algal scum on the mud and lifting it to their mouths. It's like watching Homer Simpson at an all-you-can-eat buffet. Mudskippers are in action, too, blowing bubbles and slithering across the mud with their dorsal fins raised like flags. On land, mudskippers store water in their enlarged branchial chambers, passing it slowly over their gills. When the oxygen is exhausted, they fill up again from the sea—like scuba diving in reverse. In Vietnam, mudskippers are a culinary delicacy. Sections of bamboo are buried in mudflats to create artificial burrows. After a few days they are collected, often with a skipper inside.

Fallen mangrove leaves litter the surface, soon to be dragged underground by a legion of leaf-eating crabs. The thought of all this troublesome carbon being taken out of the atmospheric game by lowly mangrove swamps gives me considerable pleasure. Ong says that when he started his carbon work, he used to stress its relevance to fisheries when seeking grant money. "Now sequestration is the thing."

The main carbon storage in mangrove forests is in the timber itself, as it is in inland rainforests, but significant extra storage happens not just in buried litter but in the roots, which in some mangroves make up almost half the total biomass of plant tissue. When these roots die in the anoxic muck of mangrove sediment, decomposition is so slow that beds of peat form that can be up to 10 meters (30-odd feet) thick.

From a climate point of view, the key to controlling the mangrove carbon asset is to keep the system intact. Disrupt it—log it, bull-doze it, drain it, burn it, plow it, build on it—and oxygen, like a predator, pounces on the unguarded carbon and drags it back into the atmosphere as CO_2.

In an ideal world, Matang's mangroves wouldn't be logged at all. Charcoal is an inefficient fuel with a high emissions price tag, and in most parts of the world it is produced unsustainably. In Matang, at least, the goal is sustainability: for every tree cut down, another is planted. Stored and released carbon approach some measure of local equity.

The wider point of Ong's work is this: even ignoring the ecolog-ical richness of mangrove forests—the multitudinous life that thrives from sea-bathed root to sunny canopy—there are compelling rea-sons to preserve and protect these forests because of the role they play in Earth's regulatory systems.

The tide is dropping. As crab burrows become uncovered, their oc-cupants emerge to begin another six-hour round of feeding and housekeeping. The tide itself is a housekeeper, bringing in food, nu-trients, and sediments and flushing out waste. Scientists describe tidal flows in mangroves as an energy subsidy—a free transportation serv-ice that not only shifts materials but also allows organisms to enter and leave the forest on a regular timetable, like shift workers.

Through the mechanism of the tides, mangroves make a vital nu-trient contribution to the wider marine ecosystem, in the form of an outwelling of dissolved organic carbon. It is as if a ship leaves the mangroves on every outgoing tide with a cargo of carbon for the oceans. Though they occupy just 0.1 percent of Earth's land surface, mangroves supply a tenth of the terrestrially derived organic carbon that is transported to the ocean.

Much of the carbon processing happens through the agency of crabs. Like Candy Feller's woodborers, mangrove crabs, especially a group called sesarmids, function as ecosystem engineers—creatures that modify the environment in ways that affect entire ecosystems.

(Other examples of ecological movers and shakers are beavers, whose tree-felling and dam-building activities restructure waterways, and termites, whose mounds are the foundations of islands in wetlands such as the Okavango Delta.) Sesarmid mangrove crabs are veritable mulching machines, devouring twice as much leaf material as they can actually assimilate. Their voluminous droppings become fodder for decomposers and detritus feeders, and by breaking down large items of vegetation such as leaves and propagules into smaller particles they accelerate the turnover of carbon and other nutrients.

The crabs also aerate and cultivate the soil, like worms in a vegetable garden. Aeration is particularly important in the oxygen-starved mangrove environment, because it prevents the buildup of ions such as sulfide and ammonium, which reduce mangrove productivity. Crab burrows perform the dual role of enabling air to penetrate the soil when the tide is out and dispersing nutrients when it is in.

Here in the feverish feeding of the mud crab and the molecular dance of organic carbon is one of the great unrecognized gifts of the mangroves: the export of nutrients to the sea. But with so few mangroves remaining, how will such vital processes be sustained? The answer, in a word, is reforestation. At the foot of Ong's scaffolding tower, I notice small boys stuffing their pockets with *Rhizophora* propagules. The forestry office will pay a few cents each for them. Ong says that throughout Asia there has been a run on propagules as countries affected by the Indian Ocean tsunami begin to replant the coastal barricades they uprooted to make space for shrimp ponds. But as I am soon to discover, there is a lot more to mangrove restoration than jamming those green, ready-to-sprout propagules into the nearest stretch of mudflat.

Chapter 10

Paradise Regained

The farm must yield a place to the forest, not as a
wood lot, or even as a necessary agricultural principle,
but as a sacred grove—a place where the Creation is
let alone, to serve as instruction, example, refuge.
—WENDELL BERRY, "The Body and the Earth"

I N THE BREAKFAST nook of the Sleep Inn, Fort Lauderdale, I
scan the smattering of early diners and correctly identify a tall
man with a long gray ponytail as my guide to the subject of
mangrove restoration. Roy "Robin" Lewis III has been rebuilding
mangrove habitats for thirty-five years. He started his academic career as an ichthyologist at the University of South Florida around
the time that two other Floridians, William Odum and Eric Heald,
were doing pioneering work on the role of mangroves in marine
ecosystems. Mangroves were disappearing fast from Florida's coastline, sacrificed for everything from condominiums to mosquito-
control impoundments. In 1975 the two ecologists wrote:

> . . . [mangroves] have been relegated to a role of botanical
> curiosities or, at best, regarded as having some slight economic
> importance as wood producers or a geological function of land
> building. At worst, they have been treated as waste land or land

that can only be improved by transformation into a garbage dump, rice field, or housing project. Roughly one-fourth of the world's tropical coastline is dominated by mangroves, and much of this is being "reclaimed" by man. For this reason it seems important to understand what value mangrove swamps possess before they are destroyed and the land which they occupy is converted to some other use.

Odum and Heald were among the first to show that, far from being ecological and economic slouches, mangroves are an important source of plant energy for the wider marine environment. In some situations they make a greater contribution to the productivity of coastal waters than seaweed or plankton.

Robin became interested, shifting his attention from fish research to wetland ecology. In the mid-1970s he formed a consultancy to advise on wetland restoration and has been working for the recovery of mangroves ever since.

He begins by telling me what restoration is not. First and foremost, it is not simply planting trees. Planting is the last phase of a process that begins with getting the topography and hydrology right. Each species of mangrove has its own preferences and tolerances in relation to tidal inundation, salinity, and other geochemical factors. If these are ignored, the plantings will fail. Do the groundwork correctly, on the other hand, and you may not have to plant at all: floating mangrove propagules will drift in and establish themselves at the optimum elevation for their species.

We take a tour through one of his project sites, West Lake Park, a 600-hectare (1,500-acre) mangrove preserve near Fort Lauderdale. A former wetland, the site had been drained to create fields for tomato growing in the early 1900s. Broward County bought the land in 1985 and hired Robin to mastermind its conversion back to mangroves. The project involved restoring saltwater flow through the site, removing invasive casuarina trees, and reshaping the land to mimic the natural topography of a mangrove wetland. Now smart boardwalks weave through lush stands of red, white, and black mangroves, the three species that occur naturally in the United States. Robin emphasizes that all of trees have seeded naturally—"volunteers," in restoration lingo. Not having to plant seedlings by hand saved the county millions of dollars.

It takes about thirty years for restored sites to achieve the stature and density of natural mangrove stands, Robin says, but the goal of ecological restoration (as opposed to reforestation) is not a nice spread of trees but functional equivalency between the restored site and a natural site. That means that all the ecological components are present, both above and below ground. In a healthy mangrove ecosystem, the total biomass can be huge. Researchers have found that a typical cubic meter of mangrove mud contains between 20,000 and 40,000 visible organisms—critters bigger than half a millimeter in size.

We stop to watch the courtship rituals of small fish called sailfish mollies, which are circling in the muddy water under the mangrove canopy. The males have a bright blue patch on their tails, which they are flashing to the females. Robin says it takes as little as five years for fish populations in restored mangroves to match those of undisturbed ecosystems, if a well-planned network of tidal creeks is included in the design. Looking at the swirling mollies, I remark, "If you build it, they will come."

But getting the chance to build doesn't come easily or often. Despite having engineered the restoration of more than thirty sites in the United States and the Caribbean, and lectured around the world on the subject, Robin says he is hardly being run off his feet with requests. "Mangroves aren't high on the conservation priority list. When it comes to marine protection, coral reefs take all the oxygen out of the room. It's the charismatic megafauna mind-set at an ecosystem level."

Coral reefs need protection, without a doubt. Warming, acidifying oceans threaten their very existence. But they have not been depleted at anywhere near the rate mangroves have. "Global loss of mangroves has been running at 1 to 2 percent a year for the past three decades," says Robin. "Imagine if we were to set a goal of no net loss of mangroves from now on. Given the current estimate of a little under 150,000 square kilometers [58,000 square miles] of mangroves worldwide, we would need to see the successful restoration of 150,000 hectares [370,000 acres] of mangroves a year to keep pace with the decline. We're not even at a hundredth of that level."

At least some of the restoration could happen in abandoned shrimp ponds. The cycle of cultivation and abandonment—the "roving banditry" of which the industry stands condemned—has left hundreds of thousands of hectares of derelict ponds along tropical shores. Natural regeneration cannot be counted on to rehabilitate this land—at least not in the short term. When ponds are abandoned, the soil dries out and becomes baked like a brick. Sulfur compounds, long buried in the anoxic mangrove mud, are oxidized through exposure to the air, making the land acidic and inimical to plant growth, even that of hardy mangroves.

Restoring water movement to the site with ditches and channels can reverse the changes. "Seawater is the world's best buffer," says Robin. "Natural flushing of an abandoned pond neutralizes the acid quickly." In a restoration trial in an abandoned shrimp pond in Costa Rica, he found that within ten years the site had achieved two-thirds of the biodiversity of an unmodified forest.

Potential restoration land is certainly available, the methodology is proven—so what's the holdup? Cost is one factor. The West Lake project cost $6 million—$10,000 per hectare, or roughly $4,000 per acre—though most of that cost was in removing exotic casuarinas and reshaping the land. Restoration of an abandoned shrimp pond within a former mangrove zone would require far less work. Robin says successful ecological restoration in developing countries can be achieved for $100 per hectare ($40 per acre).

But there are few takers. Certainly not the shrimp farmers who cleared the forests in the first place. In most countries there is no legal requirement for the aquaculture industry to restore abandoned ponds.

Rather, most replanting schemes rely on the voluntary participation of the coastal communities most affected by mangrove loss—and, by implication, most likely to benefit from their reinstatement. Understandably, villagers are not eager to donate their labor to replant mangroves unless they have some say in the long-term control, use, and management of those forests. Once bitten, twice shy. Many replanting projects have failed because they did not seek the participation or address the concerns of the local stakeholders.

A further problem is that even when rehabilitation of depleted or destroyed mangrove sites is undertaken, it is usually "rehabilitation lite"—basic reforestation rather than full-scale restoration. In a way, mangrove replanting is a victim of its own apparent simplicity. What could be easier than jabbing a mangrove propagule into the mud? Mangrove planting is sometimes seen as a fun community activity rather than a professionally planned venture. In the Philippines, for example, planting mangroves is often a festive adjunct to sand-castle competitions and beauty pageants.

Planting mangroves has even become an official Guinness World Records activity. The current record of 541,176 mangrove propagules planted by a team of 300 people within a twenty-four-hour period was set in July 2009 by the Pakistan Ministry of the Environment. That plantathon, on mudflats near the mouth of the Indus River, surpassed the previous record of 447,874, set a month earlier by an Indian army regiment in Assam. What next—the Mangrove World Series?

Half a million seedlings is nothing compared to what Senegal achieved in a recent mass planting. Between August and November 2009, a Senegalese environmental group organized the planting of 34 million seedlings by 78,000 volunteers, who responded to posters urging them to "Become a superhero! Plant your mangrove today!" The project was funded by a French dairy multinational as part of its carbon offset program.

What tends to be overlooked is whether such plantings succeed in producing viable forests. Many fail, and fail dismally, because seedlings are planted too high or too low on the shore, outside their ecological range. "The central factor in restoration is topography," says Robin. "If the elevation is too high, the site won't be flooded often enough. Too low, and it will be flooded too often. There's a sweet spot that you need to identify for each species. Get it wrong, and the seedlings will die. People have spent millions of dollars planting mangroves on mudflats, and they wonder why they fail. I'm mystified by this attitude. I could be polite and say they're misinformed, or I could be impolite and say they're stupid. You don't have to be a rocket scientist to know there's going to be a sweet spot between a mudflat and a salt pan." In restoration, as in real estate, the secret is location.

Even if a planting succeeds, its ecological value will be limited if (as is usually the case) it is a single-species monoculture. The hole in nature's account balance left by the destruction of old-growth mangroves will not be filled by planting neat rows of easy-to-plant *Rhizophora*. Nor will such plantations meet the needs of communities that rely on the rich returns of a multispecies forest for food and livelihoods. Nor, it should be noted, are single-species coastal greenbelts of much use as storm barriers, since they lack the structural complexity needed to quell the onslaught of the sea.

Full-scale mangrove restoration languishes, says Robin, because of a lack of political and social will. "It's not on anyone's radar. There is a lot of talk, a lot of wasted effort, and little real restoration. I wish I could be more positive about the prospects for mangroves, but I can't."

The failure of governments to engage in mangrove restoration debilitates the entire marine ecosystem in ways that may not be intuitive. Robin cites as an example the lionfish invasion of the Bahamas. It's a strange and cautionary tale. Lionfish are a popular coral-reef aquarium species native to the Indo-Pacific. They look spectacular—a gaudily painted body with long, flamboyant fin rays—but they have a row of venomous spines down their backs, which they can flick like a porcupine at the unwary snorkeler or reef stroller, inflicting painful stings. The story goes that a handful of lionfish escaped into the sea in south Florida in 1992 when an aquarium tank was smashed by Hurricane Andrew. The species spread up the Atlantic seaboard and eventually crossed the Gulf Stream. Once in the Bahamas, it "took off like gangbusters," says Robin.

Lionfish are fierce predators, capable of decimating native reef-fish populations. They have few natural predators, among them the goliath grouper, a fish that can grow to a gigantic size—two meters long (seven feet) and 350 kilograms (772 pounds)—and that eats pretty much anything: stingrays, lobsters, octopus, young turtles. A goliath grouper has no problem gulping down a venomous lionfish. But, like many of the world's groupers, the species has been fished to the edge of extinction.

One way of dealing with the lionfish plague is to assist the recovery of the goliath grouper, says Robin. Groupers, like many tropical fish species, occupy different habitats at different stages of their lives. The adults are reef dwellers, while the juveniles live in the protective environs of mangrove estuaries. Restore the depleted coastlines with mangroves, he says, and a goliath of a problem could be slain.

Holding on to the gains of restoration will be a challenge in an era of rising sea levels—though it is a problem mangroves have faced before. As the seas have waxed and waned throughout geological time, mangrove distribution has shifted with them in an ecological pas de deux. When the water level rises, the increased inundation triggers a response in mangroves to produce more micro-roots, which trap sediment, collect leaf litter, and create peat. The trees hoist themselves up by the bootstraps, keeping their heads above water by building up the soil around their feet.

But there are limits to how rapidly the trees can build soil. "If the rise in sea level is one to two millimeters a year, mangroves can keep up just fine," Thomas Smith, of the US Geological Survey, tells me. "If it goes up two and a half to three millimeters a year, they probably can't."

Smith is showing me around one of his research sites—Weedon Island, a nature preserve in Tampa Bay. Around Florida, the average sea-level rise for the past century has been 2.2 millimeters per year— just within the threshold of what peat-building mangroves can accommodate. Is the rate increasing? Not recently, Smith says: "In the last twenty years, sea level in the Gulf of Mexico hasn't risen a lick."

We climb to the top of an observation tower and look across the Weedon mangroves to the smart homes and jetties of Tanglewood and Harbor Isle, bayside suburbs of St. Petersburg. If I were a homeowner here, I wouldn't be complacent about sea-level rise. The current prediction of the Intergovernmental Panel on Climate Change is for an average rise of between 0.9 and 8.8 millimeters per year over the course of this century. If the IPCC's median prediction of 4.8 millimeters per year turns out to be accurate, homeowners— and mangroves—are in trouble.

People can move to higher ground, and, to an extent, mangroves can, too. Not individually, of course, but as a forest. But here in Florida, and throughout much of their range, the mangroves' escape route has been cut off by a barrier of real estate, agricultural land, ports, golf courses, roads, and other human infrastructure. The trees are caught in a squeeze between seaward inundation and landward obstruction—between the development and the deepening blue sea. Even in the absence of human impediments, a small geological escarpment would be enough of a hurdle to effectively prevent the landward march of mangroves. It would take a supreme feat of sediment trapping to hoist them over such an obstacle.

Another snag for migrating mangroves is obtaining adequate fresh water. To cope with the stress of rising seas, most mangroves will need some freshwater input or the increasing salinity will push them into a physiological red zone. As pressure on freshwater resources intensifies around the world, mangrove wetlands are getting a decreasing share. They may be salt lovers, but even the most halophytic species cannot tolerate more than about twice the salt concentration of seawater. The optimum salinity for most mangroves is

50 percent that of seawater. Freshwater availability is a major determinant of mangrove diversity. In Australia, for example, Queensland, on the wet eastern side of the continent, has eighteen mangrove species, while arid Western Australia, at the same latitude, has only four.

The complex interplay of fresh- and saltwater influences on mangroves is being put under the microscope in Florida's Ten Thousand Islands National Wildlife Refuge, on the site of the failed South Golden Gate real estate subdivision of the 1960s. Thirty years after the scheme folded, the state of Florida started buying up the property as part of the wider Everglades restoration effort, considered the most ambitious environmental repair job in history.

The former suburban dream is now the Picayune Strand State Forest. It doesn't look like much of a forest at the moment. The roads are still there, slicing up the land into neat rectangles that look, on a satellite photo, like a batch of brownies. But soon the drainage canals will be plugged and water will seep once more across the marsh, erasing the human imprint.

Before that happens, baseline data on the hydrology of the marsh needs to be gathered, so that the environmental changes during restoration can be measured. Collecting that data for the US Geological Survey's National Wetlands Research Center in Lafayette, Louisiana, is Andy From, whose foot is pushing the gas pedal to the deck of an airboat that is roaring across a few inches of Budweiser-colored water. Andy says we're lucky to have even that much water. Southwest Florida has been suffering a drought. Until a few days ago he faced the prospect of walking to his monitoring sites in the blistering summer heat. As it is, he can pull up alongside most of them, spinning the airboat around at the final moment with a flourish of the twin rudders.

We're about 15 kilometers (9 miles) east of Marco Island. One of the first sites we visit, labeled "Brackish Center" on Andy's map, is surrounded by young frost-blasted mangrove shrubs, their foliage dead and chocolate brown. Layne Hamilton, leader of the restoration project, is pleased about this. Since freshwater flow was channeled and diverted by the Golden Gate development, the salinity of the marsh has been increasing, and as a result mangroves have been creeping inland. In the 1920s mangroves covered about 4,000 hectares of the refuge area; now they range across more than 7,000 hectares (about 18,000 acres). The restoration plan includes restricting the mangrove advance and burning some existing stands. Frost is helping by killing some of the younger plants.

Older mangroves, less frost tender, are green and flowering. Their leaves are slicked with a film of brine, exuded overnight as part of the *Avicennia*'s salt-management process. As the day heats up the brine will evaporate, making the leaves look as if they have been sprinkled with salt.

Andy's water-level recorders consist of lengths of PVC pipe sunk into the soil, with mesh-covered holes at ground level so that water can flow into them. An electronic sensor is programmed to take hourly readings. While he downloads the accumulated data to a hand-held device, Joyce Mazourek, the newly appointed refuge manager, pushes a glass tube into the soggy ground and sucks up water from three different depths to measure its salinity, temperature, and electrical conductivity (reflecting the concentration of dissolved solutes).

Andy navigates from site to site by memory and guesswork. This is his seventeenth trip, but each time the layout of the marsh is different. There is no telling which of the shallow water trails we're following form part of a viable route and which are a dead end. We're like a rat in a maze, sniffing for the electronic cheese.

Occasionally our luck runs out and the airboat comes to a literal shuddering halt. When that happens, Joyce, Layne, and I get off and wade while Andy guns the prop to full helicopter blast, waggling the rudders left and right, trying to wriggle the machine into navigable water.

By midafternoon thunderheads are moving in, blackening the sky. Andy will abort the trip if they get any nearer. "An airboat on a marsh is a lightning rod," he says. But the clouds keep their distance and we continue crisscrossing the swamp, slipping through gaps between mangrove copses and skimming across grasslands where the seedheads, snicked off by the bow of the airboat, pepper our faces.

At one site Layne finds panther footprints. As well as managing the restoration project, she leads the Florida panther recovery program. There are only about a hundred of the cats left, she says—though that's three times the number there were in the mid-1990s: "They were ready to blink out."

Inbreeding has been a major problem. When a species hits a population bottleneck, as the panther has, all kinds of debilitating diseases and deformities crop up, jeopardizing recovery. The heart of the recovery program has been to introduce the panther's close relative, the western cougar, from which it is physically indistinguishable. "We brought in eight females from Texas, and they are helping fill in the holes in the genome of the panther."

Further obstacles in the way of recovery are a disease called feline leukemia, which jumps from domestic cats to panthers, and pseudorabies, which panthers pick up by eating feral hogs and which kills them almost instantly. But Layne says the top cause of mortality is intraspecific aggression. Male panthers need about 500 square kilometers (roughly 200 square miles) of range, and if they don't get it they attack and kill the females and kittens that are part of their breeding unit.

The public hasn't exactly embraced panther recovery with open arms. It may be Florida's national animal, but it is a fearsome predator. "It will take a lot of outreach and persuasion to get communities to be comfortable with a larger panther population," Layne says.

That night, driving back to the house where we're staying, Andy suddenly shouts, "Panther!" By the time I see where he is pointing, however, the cat has slunk into the shadows. It's the first time Andy has seen one in all the years he's been coming here, and while I don't begrudge him the sighting, I can't help grousing that it follows the well-known Law of Journalist Avoidance that is part of the wildlife creed. I have to settle for photographing a panther road sign.

———

Andy monitors water levels on some of the islands along the coast as well as in the marsh. Are there 10,000 islands? Well, no. More like a few hundred. But there might as well be 10,000 for the maze of mangrove-lined bays, spits, and channels they form. I first came across this confetti landscape while scouting locations on Google Earth. With sun glinting off the water at the time the image was acquired, it was hard to tell bay from island, water from forest.

Andy gets to his island stations by speedboat, using a satellite map to figure out where he is. I'm glad I'm not navigating. Such is the uniformity of forest and hummock that there are few landscape features to use for orientation. Pre-Europeans must have had their own methods; this region has had human habitation for 7,000 years. Among the more recent groups were the Calusa people, who believed that a person has three souls, one residing in the pupil of the eye, one in the reflection in water, and one in the shadow cast by the sun.

The sun is casting some harsh shadows today, but we can't put up the Bimini shade-top because we need to duck under low-hanging mangrove branches as we search for Andy's elusive recorders. In one channel we startle a spotted ray—a jet black diamond polka-dotted with white—and watch it wing away through the muddy water. Crossing a shallow bank, we see horseshoe crabs, ancient armored arthropods that have changed little in 400 million years. The air temperature is in the 90s Fahrenheit, and I'm eyeing the water for a dip, but change my mind when a six-foot bull shark swirls around the boat. The area is known for them. They are an unpredictable species, and the turbid water rules out swimming with them. I don't want to end up a case of mistaken prey identity.

To reach one of the sites, we have to walk across an island—a reminder that there are uplands, and not just mangroves, on these keys. It's parched country. We push through scrubby vegetation, palms, sea grape trees, and the occasional gumbo limbo, called the tourist tree because its shiny red bark peels like the skin of a sunburnt beachgoer. In the 1900s a few farmers scratched out a living on these islands, boiling sugarcane syrup and cutting cords of buttonwood. When they left, hermits came, seeking a life of solitude among the woodpeckers and butterflies. The last of them was still living in Dismal Key in 1992, when Hurricane Andrew tore across Florida. Warned of the storm's approach, he built a plywood box to serve either as a hurricane shelter or a coffin, depending on how things went. He survived, but now he and his ilk have all gone from the refuge.

It's coming up to high tide, and tree-climbing *Aratus* crabs have scaled the trunks of *Rhizophora* to get away from the water. Though they are not air-breathers, and every so often need to remoisten their gills in the water, they spend most of their time in the trees scraping mangrove leaves with their sharp claws. Many of the red mangroves here have dozens of crabs on them, several meters up. I climb on the prop roots to try to photograph them, but as soon as I get within range they sidle to the opposite side of the trunk. As I move to that side they circle around the other way, tiptoeing across the bark on their ballet-dancer legs, always keeping the trunk between them and me. I keep up this game of hide-and-seek for a while, trying to trick them, feinting one way and then darting the other, but they are too nimble for me. Why wouldn't they be? It's not a game to a crab. They are prey for snakes, birds, and raccoons.

We stop for lunch. Andy has made peanut butter and jelly sandwiches for him and me, and is alarmed to see Joyce eating a fruit salad with banana in it. Bananas are traditionally bad luck on boats. "Uh oh," jokes Andy. "We're in trouble now." Joyce replies that she's been eating bananas on trips into the refuge ever since she started as manager a few months earlier, and has never had boat trouble. "But have you considered CBS—Cumulative Banana Syndrome," I say. "All that pent-up banana karma may be about to be unleashed."

I'm not sure if the bad juju was in the banana or our banter, but as we head up the Faka Union Canal to the last site of the day, the motor starts making a gnashing noise and eventually cuts out permanently. We end up paddling the last mile to the marina, past the mansions of the Port of the Islands residential development. Residents probably think we've cut the engine to increase our chances of seeing a manatee. In winter, up to 300 manatees congregate for warmth in this shallow manmade canal, but in summer they're much less common. We see a few swirls of brown water that might be manatees, but we can't be sure; the water is too murky. We pass a sign saying "Manatee Zone, Idle Speed, No Wake" and give a mock grimace: we are in excessive compliance.

I leave Florida considerably heartened. The ecological restoration efforts happening here—of both fresh- and saltwater wetlands—are impressive, and all the more laudable because they are taking place in a state so riddled with introduced species and altered landscapes that rehabilitation might be considered a pipe dream. But the flourishing mangroves of Weedon Island and West Lake Park and the freshwater revivification of the Picayune Strand show that natural systems can rebound from even the severest traumas. The keys seem to be leadership, planning, some well-targeted funding, and a lot of hard work—the same ingredients that I would find in one of the world's most remarkable landscape transformations involving mangroves: the greening of the Eritrean desert.

Chapter 11

The Road to Manzanar

None of us can save the world. But we can give it a nudge.
The particular cause is not the important thing. The working is.
—John P. Wiley Jr., *Natural High*

... and the desert shall rejoice and blossom as the rose.
—Isaiah 35:1

TWO MEN SIT on planks on the hot sands of the Eritrean desert. With a knife for a chisel and a rock for a hammer, they knock the bottoms out of empty tomato sauce cans, which lie around them in a rusting heap—discards from the Eritrean navy. Nearby, on the shores of the Red Sea, a group of women push the hollow cans into the soft sediment, forming long tin-can alleys on the mudflats, and press mangrove seeds into them. In their brightly colored dresses and shawls, the women look like tropical birds that have misplaced their forest. In fact, they are creating their own forest.

Remember the parting of the Red Sea? This is the planting of the Red Sea, the brainchild of cell biologist, cancer-drug pioneer, and humanitarian Gordon Sato. In the early 1980s, Sato's laboratory at the University of California developed Erbitux, a breakthrough drug for colorectal cancer. These days, eighty-two-year-old Sato works to cure a different disease—poverty—attacking the problem not by culturing cells but by cultivating mangroves.

Eritrea was reeling from war and famine when Sato first came here in the mid-1980s. Since water is so scarce in this part of the world, Sato wondered if he could develop some form of biosaline agriculture on Eritrea's long coastline, to help provide food for the hungry. Mangroves seemed a logical, if unconventional, choice. They occurred naturally, though patchily, along the Red Sea shore, they flourished in salt water, and camels were avid browsers of the leaves. If camels ate them, why not feed the foliage to sheep and goats? Grow enough mangroves, Sato reasoned, and you could provide food security for thousands, not to mention a source of firewood and lumber. And because of mangroves' dual citizenship of land and sea, a separate aquatic economy based on fish, shellfish, and crabs could also be created.

So, like a maritime Johnny Appleseed, he began planting—and failed. All the seedlings died. Undeterred, Sato took a closer look at Eritrea's naturally occurring mangroves and noticed they were growing mostly in *mersas,* channels where fresh water flows during the brief rains that barely dampen this desert coast. Sato reasoned that it was not the fresh water the trees needed but the minerals the water was bringing from inland—specifically nitrogen, phosphorus, and iron, elements in which seawater is deficient.

By conducting a few simple trials, Sato and a small team of helpers from the Eritrean Ministry of Fisheries determined how much of the three elements mangrove seedlings needed, and devised a low-tech method of delivery. A few weeks after the propagules are planted, a small piece of iron is buried alongside. So, too, is a sealed plastic bag filled with diammonium phosphate fertilizer, a source of nitrogen and phosphorus. Three nail holes are punched in the bag. Sato has found that a three-hole drip-feed of fertilizer gives the growing seedlings the minerals they require at the optimum rate, avoiding wastage and environmentally harmful runoff. The hollow sauce cans prevent the germinating seeds from being dislodged by waves.

Now, ten years on, close to a million mangroves are growing on the formerly treeless shores of Hargigo, an impoverished village a few kilometers from the port of Massawa. Sato calls the project Manzanar, after the World War II internment camp in the California desert where, during his teens, he and his family were relocated along with thousands of other Japanese Americans. It was the memory of older internees coaxing crops from the arid California soil that inspired him all these years later.

I walk among the trees with the satisfaction of meeting old friends. Remarkably, this is the same species we have in New Zealand, half a world away. *Avicennia marina* is a botanical globetrotter, greening shores from Auckland to Okinawa, Durban to Dubai. It is one of the most widely distributed mangroves in the world. These trees are only five years old, but many are well above head height. Their leathery leaves are flecked with salt crystals, like potato crisps. I stroke the pale green velvety coats of the ripe propagules. They are about the size of small dried apricots, and some are splitting open to show the plump cotyledons inside.

Women from the village use loppers to snip off bunches of foliage, fodder for the livestock being reared as part of the project. They bind the branches in a piece of sacking and tie the bundles to each other's backs, then walk back to the village, stooping low under the barbed-wire fence that keeps camels out of the mangrove plantings. About fifty Hargigo women are employed by the project. Prior to Manzanar, it was unthinkable that a woman in the village would find paid employment. Now, as well as being paid the equivalent of a dollar a day—enough to buy a few pounds of vegetables—they also receive a daily meal and a weekly literacy lesson.

Meriem Mohammed, in flamingo pink from her head scarf to her flip-flops, moves through the grove picking propagules. They, too, are destined to be eaten by Manzanar's sheep and goats. Surplus propagules are sun-dried and ground into a grainlike product that can be stored and fed to the stock when the trees have finished fruiting. Sato estimates that a hectare of mangroves produces three tonnes (dry weight) of propagules per year. Leaf production, measured by litter fall, is around 10 tonnes per hectare (4 tons per acre). Nutritional analysis of the leaves has shown that they contain 15 percent protein, about the same as alfalfa.

The women walk carefully, trying not to break the pneumatophores that are sprouting thickly from the mud. Barnacles and oysters have started to settle on them, and crab and winkle trails crisscross the sediment. An egret has a fish crosswise in its bill. "Nature abhors a vacuum," we were taught in biology class, and here is living proof. Plant a few trees, and you usher in an ecosystem. Build nature a house, and she makes it her home.

That home extends its influence out to sea. At the end of a long rock jetty, Ibrahim Mohammed Ibrahim peels off his shirt and winds it around his head, then steps into the water to check his net. He wades chest-deep along it, feeling the meshes for fish, and turns up a nice barracuda and a jack. He cleans them on the rocks, plunging them repeatedly, almost reverently, into the water. Farther along the jetty, barefoot boys are catching finger-sized fish. Each boy's harvest lies in a silvery heap on his flip-flops. All smiles, the boys hold some fish by their tails for a photo. Like children anywhere, happy with the catching and the catch.

Hargigo's fishers have nothing but praise for the mangrove project. Since planting began, they have started to catch herbivorous fish such as mullet. Ibrahim puts the equation simply: "No mangroves, no mullet." And the little fish that make the mangroves their home attract bigger, predatory fish—the kind that snag in Ibrahim's net and sell for good prices in the Massawa market.

In a pen on the outskirts of the village, a flock of sheep crunches mangrove propagules from a wooden trough. Sato is using these animals to fine-tune his animal husbandry. He has found that mangrove leaves and seeds, though nutritious, are not a complete stock food. Fish meal, which Sato is having made locally from fish-processing offcuts, seems to provide the missing nutrients.

Most of the ewes are carrying lambs. Simon Tecleab, Sato's assistant from the fisheries ministry, brings a sheep to him and asks,

"Sato, can you tell if this one is pregnant?" The old man looks at the animal for a moment, then at Tecleab. "I'm not that gullible," he says. "It's a ram."

Sato sits on a rock in the shade of a drooping palm. Sheep approach shyly, and he reaches out to pet them. Outside the pen, donkeys nibble in the dust, not so much grazing as wishing. The stubble of grass is so miserable and sparse it fails to impart even the faintest green tinge to the parched earth. Hargigo receives an inch of rain a year, and daytime temperatures typically soar to above 100 degrees Fahrenheit. Were it not for mangrove fodder, raising livestock here would be impossible.

We make our way back through the village, past huts that are nothing more than dusty improvisations of flattened iron, bits of cloth, and scraps of wood. Some children are jumping on a truck tire, using it for a trampoline. The walls of a ruined mosque are riddled with bullet holes. Hargigo was ravaged during the war of independence from Ethiopia, and 2,000 of its occupants massacred. In this devastated community, slowly rebuilding itself, Sato dreams of seeing a livestock pen beside every hut. He has started a microcredit program in which villagers are lent a few sheep or goats, enough to start a small flock, enabling them to reach the first rung of the development ladder. "A few goats can be the beginning of an empire," says Sato. "I want to give everyone this chance. We could plant the shorelines of the Red Sea and the Arabian Gulf with mangroves and make a huge difference to people who are suffering from poverty and hunger." Who would have imagined it: the maligned mangrove, foundation of empires.

Not everyone shares Sato's vision for mangrove proliferation. Some environmentalists have criticized the project, saying that by planting an open coastline with mangroves Sato is guilty of ecological imperialism: arbitrarily replacing one ecosystem with another. Sato's response is that at one time mangroves covered much more of Eritrea's coastline than the 15 percent they now occupy, but unsustainable cutting and camel browsing reduced the mangrove footprint. At the very minimum, Manzanar is restoring mangroves to their rightful place, he says. Sato, though, is not content with the minimum. He sees in mangroves the key not just to alleviating poverty in arid lands but to mitigating climate change across the entire tropical belt. If that entails a degree of ecological adjustment, so be it. At least it is in the direction of increased biodiversity rather than the catastrophic declines associated with mangrove removal.

"It is the duty of scientists to use science to relieve hunger and poverty," Sato tells me over a bowl of Japanese noodles in his tiny office-cum-home in Massawa. "If more of us did that, it would help overturn the political mismanagement and corruption that is the biggest cause of human misery." He has calculated that if Eritrea's 1,200 kilometers (746 miles) of coastline were planted in mangroves at a density of 1,000 trees per hectare (400 per acre), the country's economic productivity would increase by 50 percent.

Sato's work on the shores of the Red Sea has earned him the Rolex award for enterprise and the Blue Planet environmental prize. He is a member of the prestigious National Academy of Sciences and a distinguished alumnus of the California Institute of Technology. Caltech's motto is a verse from the New Testament: "The truth shall make you free." The octogenarian scientist, whose face is partly paralyzed from a stroke yet who spends several months a year working in the punishing climate of the Horn of Africa, echoes that thought when he tells me that even if the Manzanar project should end, he'll have the satisfaction of having given people life-sustaining knowledge.

The day before I arrived in Massawa, the town had celebrated the fifteenth anniversary of its liberation from Ethiopian forces—a David-and-Goliath struggle (as Eritreans tell it) in which the pride of the Ethiopian navy was bested by a ragtag band of Eritreans in speedboats. A sign on a cafe shows a soldier in a heroic pose and the slogan "Able to do what can't be done."

Out on the mudflats another old soldier is attempting the impossible: turning the tide of poverty by growing mangroves. The gardeners of Manzanar would be proud.

Chapter 12

Under the Mango Tree

The extent to which the disappearance of forests over the
coming century may be slowed, and the extent to which forests
will be effectively managed over the coming century, depends
first and foremost upon the extent to which governments
devolve their jurisdiction—and ideally ownership—
over these estates to the local level.
—LIZ ALDEN WILY, *development consultant*

*T*HE VILLAGERS OF Twasalie have gathered in the spacious
shade of an old mango tree, their traditional meeting place, to
discuss the state of the environment. In 1999, Twasalie was
one of four villages in Tanzania's mangrove-rich Rufiji Delta offered
the chance to take part in a pilot program of the World Conservation Union (IUCN), the Tanzanian government, and the Dutch
government, aimed at reducing poverty by conserving and sustainably managing natural resources.

The project came at a critical time for Twasalie. The 900-strong
community felt embattled. Outsiders were infiltrating its mangrove
forests, harvesting the timber, and appropriating the cleared land
for agriculture. Traditional fishing areas were also under pressure.
Boats were coming from long distances to harvest fish and prawns
in Twasalie's backyard. Even more worrying were government plans

to allow an aquaculture company to establish 100 square kilometers (38 square miles) of shrimp ponds in the floodplain grasslands where the villagers grow their staple crops of rice, sorghum, maize, and cassava. Oil prospectors were exploring the delta, putting in survey markers. Twasalie's resource base—indeed, its very existence— seemed under threat. Unsure of its legal rights and lacking practical methods of monitoring and enforcement, the community felt powerless to protect its lands, forests, and fisheries.

The IUCN project promised a way forward, and the village accepted the offer eagerly. Over the next four years a raft of initiatives was begun. Workshops were held on everything from beekeeping to bookkeeping, wildlife management to water pump maintenance. Lawyers from Dar es Salaam came to explain how to prepare a set of bylaws that would protect the village's natural resources. Mangrove experts assessed the state of the forests and helped produce a management plan. The village decided to close its local rivers to fishing during the spawning season, and to require outsiders to buy licenses to fish Twasalie's waters. A poultry vaccination program enabled some villagers to begin commercial chicken farming. Two women's groups opened chai shops. The school was rebuilt. The village opened a bank account and installed a radio system that not only connected it to all the hospitals and administrative centers of the district, but also enabled villagers to listen to short-wave radio stations and feel less cut off from the outside world.

Despite the gains, problems persist. The village remains unsure of its precise geographical boundaries, and disputes erupt with its neighbors over resource entitlement. This uncertainty emboldens outsiders to flout Twasalie's bylaws and to continue fishing its waters and clearing its forests. Birds and wild animals are a persistent threat to crops, requiring children to work as scarecrows instead of attending school. Despite a government moratorium on cutting mangroves in reserved forests, local authorities issue harvesting licenses.

Under the mango tree, a man who has been trained as a scout

says he is disillusioned because when he reports illicit mangrove cutting, nothing is done. Another man says that if other villages are cutting mangroves and earning money by selling the poles to traders, why should Twasalie miss out on that revenue? Someone else disagrees, saying the village should stay true to its plan to conserve its mangroves, regardless of what other villages or outsiders do. "The prawns we catch are because of the mangroves," he says. "The mangroves give us fish and shade and good air to breathe, and they stop the soil being washed away." To which another counters, "It's nice to have a shady forest, but when you need rice to feed your family you can't just admire the trees. You have to cut them down so you can plant more rice."

Opinions swirl like leaves in a dust storm. More mangrove seedlings should be planted. No they shouldn't, because other villages pull them up or burn them. Given the continuing conflict and jealousy between villages, perhaps Twasalie should never have become involved in the project, one person suggests.

The meeting breaks up when a chameleon walks conspicuously through the center of the group and starts climbing the tree, and everyone stops talking to watch. It seems for a moment that this totemic creature with its omnidirectional stare is about to say something. But if it possesses ancient wisdom, the lizard isn't sharing it with us.

The fact that I get the gist of the discussion is due to the rapid, sotto voce translations of Rose Hogan, an Irish environmental consultant who helped set up the project for the IUCN. Rose has a background in agriculture. For her degree, she wrote a thesis on the quintessentially Irish subject of potatoes. A month after handing it in, she traveled to the southern highlands of Tanzania to work on an aid project with Concern International. "At the end of the project I tried to go back to Ireland to take up some sort of career, but Africa kept drawing me back," she tells me. And it has continued to do so for twenty-five years.

For Rose, this trip is a nostalgic reunion with people she spent many months living and working with. For me, it is a chance to see how mangrove management works in an African setting. Is sustainable management possible? Are the goals of communities, governments, and outside environmental groups compatible? Much of our visit focuses on the people of the delta and the deep challenges they face. Rose tells me about an incident early on in her work that made her aware of the motivational paralysis that a lifetime of powerlessness produces. She was asking a group of Twasalie women what skills or training they would like to have. They looked at her blankly. Aspiration was a foreign concept to them. Eventually they suggested that if a few of them could learn to be boat drivers they wouldn't have to rely on men to take their goods to market, and they wouldn't have to worry about the men shortchanging them or spending the proceeds. Also, if they had more control over transportation, they could visit a medical clinic if they or their children were sick.

Salima Salamala was one of four women who received training to be a boat driver. On our journey through the delta we visit her in her rice field, where she lives in a stilt house with her children. She is married to a man who has two other wives. During the rice-growing season, she rarely sees him. Like most women in the delta, she stays with her children in the floodplains until the crop is harvested. A few weeks before our visit, her youngest child contracted cholera. The disease often breaks out at the beginning of the rainy season. Fortunately, a medical team was passing. They stayed several days, rehydrating the child and nursing her through the worst of the bout.

What about the boat, I ask. She became a driver for just this sort of emergency. Could she not have taken the child to a clinic? Life is not that simple. Her field is far from the village center, where the boat is kept, and there is no means of communication. By the time she reached Twasalie, her daughter might already have succumbed. In any case, decisions on boat use are made by the village hierarchy, and she says her interests and suggestions are often ignored.

Salima says proudly that she is "an environmental woman," and shows us the mangroves she has planted around her field to reduce erosion and serve as a future timber resource for her children. Blue-backed fiddler crabs scuttle around the bases of the rice plants. Before the environmental project began, villagers used DDT and other pesticides to kill the crabs. Now they remove them by hand, accepting a degree of crop damage for the sake of the health of the soil and waterways.

Rose tells me that women like Salima are her inspiration. "They take their training and chances seriously," she says. "What they need is long-term assistance. Many development projects end too quickly. It's like giving a child a single year of schooling and expecting them to be fully educated."

Another moment of clarity: when Rose was working in Twasalie, she asked the women to draw a picture of their most cherished dream. One drew a chair under a tree. Bliss for her was simply a chance to rest. The yoke of work presses hard on the women of Twasalie. During the fasting month of Ramadan, women work nineteen hours a day, girls fourteen hours . . . and men five.

We spend a sweltering night in tents on the bank of the River Bumba. What little sleep I manage to pry from the jaws of an over-active consciousness is punctuated by the grunts of hippos, the howls of jackals, and the hootings of owls.

In the morning we walk into the mangroves. Every mangrove forest is different, even down to the sound the mud makes as you walk. Some mud sounds like sticky tape being ripped from a roll. Other mud produces a deep, resonant slurp. This mud, pocked with crab holes and spiked with pneumatophores, causes jets of water to squirt up our legs with every step.

We disturb a six-foot snake that promptly slides into a hollow tree trunk. Fragments of whitened crab shell lie on a nearby stump—the remains of a Sykes monkey's meal. Sykes monkeys are crab specialists. According to Mohamedi, the boat driver, they use their long tails like fishing lures. A monkey will lower its tail into a crab burrow, he says, wait for the crab to nip it, then pull its tail out with the crab attached. It seems incredible: Brazilian raccoons and Tanzanian monkeys using the same technique to capture crabs. Regrettably, the monkey I am looking at is not engaged in crab angling; it is sitting on a log. It has a tan back, a white mane, and hooded gray eyebrows that look like wire brushes. Squirrels chatter in the branches overhead.

As we travel downriver we pass several *mamba*, crocodiles, floating near the bank. One is feeding on the bloated carcass of a wild pig. Mohamedi says a crocodile once snapped the blade of his canoe paddle in its jaws. "Ate it as you would eat a chapati," he says.

We stop to watch a woman catching freshwater shrimp using a pole trap called a *dema*. A piece of cloth, sewn into a bag shape, is attached to a long pole. The mouth of the bag is kept open by a circle of woody vine. The device looks like an upside-down lampshade with the top closed off. She throws a handful of rice bran into the trap and lowers it into the river at the edge of her rice field. After a few minutes she pulls it up and shows us several plump white shrimp kicking and jumping in the bottom of the bag.

Late in the afternoon we reach Kibanju, a fishing port built in the mangroves where the Bumba meets the Indian Ocean. At the peak of the prawn-fishing season 4,000 people squeeze into the place, living in huts on stilts. The alleys, paved with mangrove logs, disappear under water when the spring tides come.

Fishers are returning from sea, hauling their canoes up the slippery mud in front of the town and tossing their catches of fish and prawns into buckets. On a veranda, a man chews a stalk of sugarcane. Opposite him a teenage girl grates coconut flesh while her boyfriend smokes a cigarette.

We find a teahouse and order a meal of fish, rice, and chapatis. How do you cook on an open fire when the floor of your house is made of mangrove poles? The proprietor takes me behind a partition into the kitchen to see. A mat of woven palm fronds positioned near a window opening has been packed with mud and sand. River stones on top of the hardened mud support the pots and pans, and a few sticks of firewood stand ready to feed the glowing flames. I watch as she boils the pieces of fish in coconut milk, then shifts them into hot oil for frying.

Wherever you go in the Rufiji, you see the blue smoke of cooking fires rising through thatched roofs. Firewood is the only readily available fuel, and each household uses close to four tonnes a year. Salt making also consumes a huge amount of timber: seven tonnes of firewood to produce one tonne of salt. There are eight species of mangrove in the Rufiji (not counting the mangrove fern) and all are used for firewood, though most have an additional suite of uses: *Heritiera* for dhow planks, keels, booms, and masts; *Sonneratia* for windows, doors, beehives, and household furniture (and *Sonneratia* pneumatophores for net floats); *Bruguiera* for fishing stakes and poles; *Avicennia* for building short-lived canoes (two to three years), smoking fish, evaporating salt, and firing pottery kilns; *Xylocarpus* for long-lived canoes (up to ten years), dhow ribs, and a fish toxin; *Rhizophora* for black cloth dye and fish traps; *Ceriops* for red cloth dye and fence posts.

Several species have medicinal and cultural uses as well: *Avicennia* sap for earache; the seeds of the heavy, cannonball-sized fruit of *Xylocarpus* for stomach upsets and in worship rituals. Mangrove honey is a medicine for both body and soul: it treats stomach complaints and mouth ulcers, exorcises evil spirits, and is part of the ceremony that ushers children into the Muslim faith.

In a thatched shelter in the middle of a rice field I watch a boatbuilder with the muscles of a boxer adzing the deck struts of a dhow. Wine-red shavings fall from the blade and gather in the hull. Every timber in the vessel is mangrove wood, he says as he picks up a bowstring drill and begins the laborious task of boring a hole in the dense timber.

Dhows built from mangrove timber have been carrying mangrove cargoes out of East Africa for 2,000 years. Mangrove poles, prized for their strength and termite resistance, were the two-by-fours of the Arabian building industry. The mud roofs of Oman and Basra were supported by the mangrove rafters of Zanzibar and Rufiji. Dhows sailed from the Persian Gulf to Africa during the northeast monsoon, bringing dates, carpets, and earthenware, and returned during the southeast monsoon with poles, firewood, and mangrove bark for tanning. The mangrove pole trade was so important that each grade of pole had its own name—from spindly inch-thick *fito*, used by the hundreds as reinforcing rods in the mud walls of traditional Swahili houses, to foot-thick *vigingi*, used as load-bearing girders in multistory buildings.

There are an estimated 500 square kilometers (195 square miles) of mangrove forest in the Rufiji Delta, making it the largest mangrove expanse in East Africa. But the combined pressure of the commercial pole trade, local cutting for firewood, and construction and clearance for agriculture has depleted the forests alarmingly. The challenge of making the mangrove harvest sustainable has vexed the Tanzanian government for decades. In 1987, it took the draconian step of imposing a moratorium on all mangrove cutting. But enforcement in remote, labyrinthine Rufiji was impossible, and both subsistence cutting and commercial trading continued.

The ban soured the relationship between coastal villagers and mangrove administrators because it showed how out of touch officialdom was. To prohibit mangrove cutting was to inflict a sentence of starvation. By one village's estimate, 75 percent of their income came directly from mangroves, with the rest from fishing and farming.

A government-ordered mangrove management study in 1991 acknowledged the problem. The government had failed to appreciate the complexity and importance of the resource, its authors wrote. It had focused on controlling the mangrove timber export trade and "not on the essential role of mangroves in supplying the basic needs of coastal communities or their important value to fisheries." The report arrived at a conclusion that had hitherto eluded officials: mangrove management must include the participation of the people who rely on the resource. Instead of managing the delta as a national reserve, with a one-size-fits-all regimen of licenses and prohibitions, the government should allocate areas for local communities to manage and control.

Among other benefits, this would change the power relationship between traders and villagers. "Instead of a trader with his license to cut seeking the cheapest labor, it will now be the local people seeking the highest price for poles from several traders," noted the report. "Until such a scheme is effected, the price of mangrove poles will not reflect the true cost of managing the mangroves."

In 1997, Tanzania enacted a new forest policy that allowed the possibility of collaborative management. It was this legislative change that opened the way for the IUCN projects in Twasalie and its sister villages. Tanzania and The Gambia have been pioneers in participatory forest management in Africa, but other nations have been quick to follow their lead. Liz Alden Wily, a British consultant on land tenure and community forestry management, says that more than thirty African countries have now launched community forest initiatives—an impressive achievement, given that almost no such management regimes existed on the continent in the mid-1990s.

Around the world, participatory forest management has flourished as conventional top-down, regulation-based governance has proved unable to arrest declining biodiversity or sustain the subsistence communities that rely on forest resources. There is growing recognition that the best custodians of natural resources may be the people whose lives and livelihoods depend on them.

The conservation benefit of community ownership, says Wily, arises from the fact that the forest is no longer thought of as merely a resource to exploit but as an asset to be protected. Like any capital asset, its preservation allows a sustainable stream of benefits to flow. It is a win-win outcome for people and planet.

But the power sharing has to be real, and not just lip service. As Wily notes, state bureaucracies tend to let go of the levers of control only reluctantly. In many so-called joint forest management initiatives, the community partner is expected to shoulder most of the operational responsibilities but is given few of the powers to determine who may or may not use the forest and under what conditions, and to license and enforce accordingly. In these situations, she says, "communities usually serve less as decision-makers than those consulted, less as regulators than rule-followers, less as licensing authorities than licensees and less as enforcers than reporters of offences to still-dominant government actors."

In Twasalie, these were some of the concerns that emerged in the discussion under the mango tree. The mechanisms may not be perfect, but Tanzania's community-managed mangroves, like the *custodias* of Ecuador and the extractive reserves of Brazil, point to improved prospects for both the forests and their users.

Chapter 13

A City and Its Mangroves

It is virtually impossible to find a mangrove swamp
anywhere on the planet that has not been altered
substantially by human activities.
—Aaron Ellison, *Harvard forest ecologist*

*T*HE *ASIAN EXCELSIOR* is sinking slowly in front of my eyes.
Two pairs of electric "mules" have just towed the big black cargo
ship into the Miraflores Locks, and now, as the surface of the
Panama Canal burns orange in the sunset, she drops inch by inch
with the water in the first lock.

Watching with me from the balcony of the Miraflores visitor center are Rosabel Miró and her husband, Karl Kaufmann. They are
bird people by inclination. Rosabel, a native Panamanian, is the director of the Panama Audubon Society. Karl, an American who has
lived in Panama for thirty years, is an environmental data manager
with the Smithsonian Tropical Research Institute. Panama's 950
bird species give them plenty of scope for observation and discovery. But in recent years they have become mangrove defenders
as well. They had no choice, they say. Mangroves are vital to the
ecology of many of the migratory shorebirds that fill the skies
around Panama City. To care about birds is to care about the habitats that sustain them.

An orange-hulled container ship slips out of the last lock and steams toward the Pacific. "The next TV you buy may have spent some time on an old mangrove site," says Karl. "Panama grew up on the edge of mangroves. Mangroves are part of its heritage. But today's city is turning its back on them in favor of golf courses and recreational areas."

I have come to Panama City to see how this metropolis of more than one million people lives with its mangroves. I want to find out if it's possible to accommodate growth without irreparably damaging natural assets. Panama's economy is booming. When the country gained ownership of the canal in 1999, it was like being handed a cash cow. Panama City itself is now bursting at the seams. In some neighborhoods the population density reaches 35,000 per square kilometer (90,000 per square mile). The city's growing pains are those of any burgeoning urban center—"too many cars, too few roads, a big mess every morning," says Rosabel. But expansion here is harder than in other areas. Panama City is squeezed between the canal to the west and mangrove forests to the east. These forests have the highest diversity of mangroves in the Americas—twelve species—and in February 2009 they were declared a protected area. But will protection on paper save the trees on the ground? The pressure to build on and around mangrove land is intense.

Before we visit the urban mangroves, Rosabel wants to show me Panama's first mangrove conservation project, located an hour southwest of the city in Chame, a mangrove-fringed estuary shaped like a fish's mouth. Two staff from Panama's national environmental authority, ANAM, the Autoridad Nacional del Ambiente, join us.

We set out early in the morning, taking the Pan-American Highway through towns where fruit stalls jam the sidewalks and bakeries beckon. I haven't eaten breakfast, and am grateful when we stop for cheese-filled empanadas and *chicheme,* a refreshing cold drink that consists of corn kernels mixed with sweet, thickened milk.

A little farther down the road we stop again for a group of environmental campaigners who are handing out pamphlets and posters to travelers. They hold banners saying *Salvemos el planeta* (Let's save the planet) and *Convivamos con el bosque* (Let's live with the forest). They are an enthusiastic group, chatting and laughing with drivers and passersby, climbing aboard Panama's gaudily painted buses—artworks on wheels, really—to give pamphlets to the passengers.

As he drives, ANAM's José Berdiales explains the Chame project. The Bay of Chame is home to four coastal communities that depend heavily on mangroves. Three hundred families earn a living by cutting mangrove poles for construction or converting mangrove logs into charcoal, relying in addition on the fish and shellfish that the mangrove ecosystem provides.

In 2004, the environmental authority became concerned about the pressure being placed on the mangroves. A survey found that at least 100 charcoal kilns were in operation, each consuming fifteen to twenty mangrove trees per month. Pole cutters were taking 100 trees per month. "The forest could not support so many people cutting so much," José says.

With financial backing from the International Tropical Timber Organization, ANAM set up a project to manage and conserve 4,000 hectares (about 10,000 acres) of mangroves in the Chame watershed. Some areas have been declared off limits to cutting, some are being replanted, and some are to be used in agroforestry.

José drives up a steep side road for a panoramic view over the Bay of Chame. There is a sharp line where the verdant green of farmland meets the somber tones of the mangroves, which bulge inland from the coast in a 6,000-hectare (14,000-acre) crescent. "These are the most heavily utilized mangroves in Panama," José says. He wants to see the harvest become sustainable—especially for the red mangrove, which is the favored species for both poles and charcoal. A few shrimp ponds pock the expanse of forest. Most of them are abandoned, says José. The Panamanian government stopped granting concessions for shrimp farms sited in mangroves in 2006.

At the village of Espave we turn down a dirt track that ends at the mangroves. White smoke billows around a man who is shoveling soil onto a cone-shaped mound. He shovels and then pats down the black peat, working his way around the mound, which is about three meters (10 feet) high and shaped like a wigwam. The wind changes and blocks him from view for a few moments; then he reappears, still shoveling and patting.

He is a *carbonero*, a charcoal maker, and he is sealing up the ventilation holes in an earth kiln, lit just hours ago. The mound, known as a *horno*, will smolder for six days, by which time the transformation from mangrove to charcoal will be complete. Another *horno*, yet to be covered with soil, stands nearby, as intricately constructed as a dry-stone wall. One of the *carboneros*, shirtless and powerfully built, tells us they use a fifty-fifty mix of red and white mangroves. Each *horno* yields between seventy and eighty sacks of charcoal.

At a newly cleared site, a young man unloads freshly cut mangrove logs from a pink wheelbarrow on which someone has painted the words *mi paloma*—my dove—and a heart. It seems an odd name for a wheelbarrow, not to mention an unusual sentiment.

A truck arrives to collect poles. The red mangrove poles have been debarked, but white mangrove poles are sold bark-on. José tells me that in the north of Panama, near the Costa Rican border, there is a group of *mangleros* (mangrove workers) who specialize in debarking red mangroves for the tanning trade. These *cascareros* take only mature trees, trees so large it would take two people linking arms to reach around the trunk. The timber is wasted because the bark cutters lack the capacity to transport the trunk to a mill. This practice is on ANAM's list of concerns, but because the harvest is small—perhaps eighty trees a month—it is being allowed to continue for now.

When the Chame project began, some of the local people protested that the environmental authority had no right to interfere with their livelihood. The task of winning their cooperation—or at least quelling their opposition—fell to Juliana Chavarria, a soft-spoken young ANAM staffer who explains some of the challenges she faced. "Some of the people weren't happy about the restrictions placed upon them," she says. "They believe the mangroves will never end." Juliana realized she needed to find ways to demonstrate a short-term positive outcome for the communities and their forests. For mangrove workers, the "win" that would have the biggest impact was more money in the pocket.

She came up with a scheme that is starting to show such a bottom-line return: the production and marketing of "eco-charcoal." Ordinarily, *carboneros* get $2 for a 35-pound sack from a distributor who sells to restaurants, merchants, and other users in Panama City. Juliana negotiated with a supermarket chain and found that the same quantity of charcoal would sell for $13 if it were repackaged in 8-pound lots and carried a label saying that it was harvested sustainably. Most importantly, the supermarket buyer was willing to deal directly with the *carboneros*. "Everyone benefits," she tells me. "The *carboneros* get more money, the supermarket stocks a quality product, and the consumer has the satisfaction of supporting a sustainable harvest."

Juliana shows me a small nursery of sprouting mangrove propagules. The seedlings are potted in black polythene bags, and each has two leaves, like a pair of ears, at the top of a stout green stem. When they have six leaves they will be ready for planting, she says. Reforestation in Espave began in 2005, and the replanted stands are already more than two meters (seven feet) tall. Initially, ANAM taught community members how to select and store propagules, how to grow them, how and when to plant, and which tidal elevation suits which species. Now, Juliana says, the community does it all without outside help. The work is paid for by ANAM, and there are revenue opportunities as well. ANAM pays $10 for 1,000 propagules. Once a community has a nursery up and running, it can supply seedlings to its neighbors.

We drive to another *horno* site beside a tidal creek. A few sheets of roofing iron form a shelter near a concrete pad where the mound is built, but there is nobody around, and only blackened ashes on the pad. When the *carboneros* make charcoal here they stay for the duration of the burn, monitoring the heat of the pile and the amount of oxygen getting to it. Surveillance is critical. If the *horno* catches fire, all the work goes up in smoke.

Charcoal making Chame-style is a far simpler proposition than the factory-like process I witnessed in Malaysia, with reusable brick kilns in a continuous firing sequence, and everything under cover. But the supply issue is the same: if the industry doesn't grow as much new timber as it takes, it has no long-term future.

Several dozen sacks of charcoal stand on the landing, ready to be collected by boat. I unlace the top of a sack and pull out a few crisp, gray lumps. It's not the eco-friendliest fuel on earth, but if its production can be made sustainable, that will be a step forward for Panama's mangroves.

After I visit the conservation project, Rosabel Miró wants me to see the darker side of Panama's economic boom. We set out for a new area of coastal development near Juan Díaz, on the eastern fringe of Panama City. To get there we drive past the crumbling stone walls of Panama Viejo, Old Panama, sacked by the pirate Henry Morgan in 1671, then through the upscale residential area of Costa del Este, then past a sign announcing "Santa Maria Golf and Country Club" to the development site itself, where bulldozers are at work.

Rosabel is concerned because the site is within an area that was declared a protected area in February 2009, and because the continued nibbling away of mangroves poses a threat to shorebirds. "The Bay of Panama is the most important stopover for migratory shorebirds in Central America," she tells me. Two million shorebirds of more than thirty species, including plovers, sandpipers, and whimbrels, use the area. One reason they stop here is the huge tides on the Pacific coast—up to seven meters (23 feet) of difference between high and low. When the tide goes out, it exposes a vast acreage of mudflat—a huge open-air shorebird buffet.

Mangroves are important to shorebirds not just because of nutrient interactions between mudflat and mangrove forest, and the influence this has on food supply, but also because they provide safe roosting sites and a security buffer between the birds' territory and urban areas inland.

The new development is mostly inshore of the mangrove belt, but given mangroves' sensitivity to hydrological changes, eutrophication, and pollution, interference with the watershed can be as damaging as outright deforestation.

Rosabel believes a stand must be taken. Her organization has been working for the creation of the Bay of Panama protected area, and for mangrove conservation in general, for a decade. In 2008, the conservation cause received a boost when the Panamanian government decreed that all mangroves were "special management areas," recognizing their role in hydrology, ecology, coastline protection and stabilization, as well as their public use. Leslie Marín, a law student and a member of Rosabel's staff, read me some of the clauses from the legislation. "It is illegal to cut, use, commercialize or reduce the area of mangroves without permission. It is illegal to modify the land or its hydrology, to build on it or use any parts of it." It is a good law, he says, but there is still debate over who has jurisdiction over mangroves. "We have a law here, a resolution there. Local mayors can take matters into their own hands, ignoring national protections. We need a single powerful mangrove law, and implementation at the highest level."

Included in the recent legislative changes are valuations and penalties relating to mangrove loss. Where mangrove removal is deemed a public necessity, the land is valued at $20,000 per hectare ($8,100 per acre). If the removal is for a commercial project, the price goes up to $150,000 per hectare. If mangroves are removed illegally, the fine is $300,000 per hectare.

Such valuations are an advance over the assumption that mangroves are a free commons—or a wasteland—though Karl Kaufmann believes there is an inherent flaw with the valuation approach. "If you put a dollar value on mangroves, it's an incentive to sell. You're taking a public asset—the goods and services that mangroves have provided for hundreds of years—and putting it up for grabs in a one-time sale. And it isn't even the people who rely on mangroves who get reimbursed for the loss of the asset, it's the government."

A better approach, Karl thinks, is one in which for every hectare of mangroves taken, a hectare is replanted. Even though there is a short-term loss of mangrove benefits, at least the public good is perpetuated for future generations.

The Bay of Panama protected area includes an almost unbroken band of mangroves stretching from the outskirts of Panama City for 100 kilometers (62 miles) eastward along the coast. Rosabel and her colleagues are working to develop a conservation strategy for the area, which they hope will be incorporated in the management plan. They expect battles ahead. Nearly half a million hectares (more than a million acres) of land near the protected area is under consideration for mining and residential development, and a further 40,000 hectares just offshore is subject to applications for the extraction of rock and sand. The protected area is going to need sharp legal teeth to fend off developers whose activities threaten its ecological integrity.

Rosabel drives to the end of the road, where it meets the mouth of the Juan Díaz River. We notice a cluster of ramshackle huts standing on a scrap of land between mangroves and a sheet-metal works that is turning out sections of tailrace tunnel for a hydroelectric project. I'm curious to know who is living there, so we take a path that brushes past young banana palms and papaya trees and meet the residents: Antonio, Magdalena, Lisbeth, and Vijil. They invite us to share the shade of an old almond tree. While we swing in fishing-net hammocks, they talk about their life here. They and a few others drifted together by happenstance, they say, much like mangrove propagules cast up on a beach. They have fashioned a simple, if not entirely idyllic, existence on the shores of the bay. The fact that they wake in the morning to the sound of arc welders and angle grinders is a small price to pay for a life close to nature and far from the crowded city.

They grow vegetables in what looks to my eye to be friable, fertile soil. Magdalena shows off a huge pumpkin that will be used as bait in the crab traps they set at low tide. Like all subsistence communities, they know the bounty that each season brings. November is when the iguanas come, for instance—"cooking time," Vijil says with a grin. I follow Antonio a few steps into the mangroves, where he uses a table knife to dig up shellfish from around the trunks of the trees. It isn't the mangrove cockle of Ecuador, but a much smaller bivalve that lives in sandier conditions. Antonio says they're tasty, but you need a lot of them for a meal.

Hens scratch among piles of empty soft drink and beer cans washed ashore by the tide. A scrap metal merchant comes by from time to time and pays a few dollars for the aluminum. Lisbeth, an older woman, collects parakeet chicks in the mangroves during the breeding season, raises them to fledging size, and sells them in the city for $3 each. She brings out a pet parakeet and a large green parrot, which perches on Rosabel's finger and starts to sing—"sing" being a generous description of its vocal performance. This bird is all beak and no voice box. Rosabel grew up with a succession of pet parakeets. "We called them all Juanito or Juanita," she says. She and the neighboring children used to go adventuring in the mangroves beside her house, so she has a warm feeling for this little band of urban refugees living their *Swiss Family Robinson* life.

Antonio tells us there's an old crab collector living deep in the mangroves on the other side of the river, and offers to take us to meet him at high tide the next morning. I'm keen for another opportunity to observe a mangrove-centered life. It's a deal, we say. We'll bring breakfast for the community, and Antonio and Vijil will paddle us across the river to meet the old man of Juan Díaz.

We return to the city, and that evening Karl Kaufmann and I head for the suburb of Diablo to look for *Pelliciera*, Candy Feller's magic mangrove. Karl remembers seeing it here in the past, in a little patch of forest beside some boatyards, sheds, and rickety wharves. We've witnessed mangrove conservation in Chame and the threat of encroaching development in Juan Díaz, but I'm still curious about the possibility of urban mangroves, plucky survivors holding the line.

Diablo lies in the former Canal Zone, a corridor of land that extended five miles on each side of the Panama Canal. It's a leafy neighborhood of spacious weatherboard duplex houses that were characteristic of the zone, an administrative entity that came to an end in 1999 when the canal passed to Panamanian control. Karl, a fount of historical knowledge, says city officials became unhappy with the name Diablo and changed it—diametrically, one might say—to Altos de Jesus, Heights of Jesus. But the residents objected. Signs with the new name kept disappearing, and eventually the name change was given up as a lost cause.

We walk down a boat ramp and, with the high tide lapping at our ankles, wade into the mud. Before long we spot the distinctive splayed roots and star-shaped flowers we have been hoping to see. Flies are crawling over the spathes of unopened blooms, searching for a way to reach the nectar inside. Here on the Pacific coast, *Pelliciera* flowers are much pinker than they are on the Caribbean side, at Bocas del Tora, and the senescent leaves turn scarlet rather than yellow. Candy Feller suspects they are two distinct species.

There's something appealing about finding a treasure like *Pelliciera* in a neglected backwater in a township called Diablo. It's one of the reasons I became interested in mangroves in the first place. They're maligned, they're marginalized, they're considered unpleasant and creepy—Steinbeck's foul-smelling forests of stalking, quiet murder. Documentary makers aren't beating a path to the mangroves; their eyes are on more charismatic ecosystems, such as Amazonian rainforests and coral reefs. I have nothing against these habitats, but they've become ecological celebrities. Mangroves are underdogs. Poking around in mangroves is like looking for gold in unexpected places.

As arranged, Karl, Rosabel, and I return to the camp by the Rio Juan Díaz the next morning. High tide is heaving a flotsam of trash in slow, rhythmic waves. The Bay of Panama should be called the Bay of Garbage. Household rubbish floats down the rivers, and the tide distributes it along the beaches and up into the mangroves. We walk through it up to our knees to get to the canoe, a stumpy dugout that looks in danger of capsizing even before we get in, let alone once we start across the channel.

Vijil paddles the clunky craft to the opposite shore, where we set out to find the old *cangrejero*. We follow a trail under stands of tall *Avicennia*, where pelicans, cormorants, frigate birds, and vultures are roosting for the duration of the high tide. The undergrowth is so spattered with guano that it looks as if someone with a paint gun has run amok. The stench of ammonia is intense. Pelicans hoist themselves off the swaying branches and wing across the bay, rising and falling against the distant skyscrapers of downtown Panama City.

We slosh through the mud, the snorkel roots, and the trash. We are at least 100 meters from the shore now, but light bulbs, plastic bottles, and flip-flops lie in thick drifts among the trees. Among the more ubiquitous items of garbage, I notice a Mickey Mouse Frisbee, a deflated basketball, and, as if placed deliberately, a woman's sandal supported six inches above the mud on mangrove pneumatophores. It looks like Cinderella's slipper, awaiting a foot. On a patch of drier ground I find several cactuses growing among the mangrove roots—the first time I have seen this plant combination.

Antonio finds the path. It winds through tall canal grass—an invasive species that grows head-high on thick stalks. In a few minutes we reach the crabber's camp. There are hot embers smoldering under a pot, but the crabber is nowhere to be seen. Vijil and Antonio whistle and call, but there is no response. They walk into the forest to look for him. A puppy yawns and stretches in a patch of sunlight. I notice a pile of homemade crab traps lying under a tree.

Our guides return, disappointed. "He must have gone hunting," they say. We decide not to wait. The tide falls so quickly on this coast that if we don't go soon we will not be able to cross the river until evening. We leave a bag of rice for the *cangrejero* of Juan Díaz and retrace our steps. Even now the tide has retreated by hundreds of meters, leaving a brown silt soup below the wrack line.

It is fitting that my visit to Panama should end in a mangrove forest that is both a cornucopia and a rubbish heap. Juan Díaz epit-omizes the global mangrove problem: they are treasured by the few and trashed by the many. How is that situation to be turned around? Karl Kaufmann believes we need a new narrative about land use. We're clinging to an illusion, he says, if we think of land as a col-lection of private, discrete assets—this piece mine, that piece yours. "From the point of view of the earth, my plot of land isn't separate from everyone else's. We all have a stake in what's left."

This is Ecology 101. As Barry Commoner, US biologist and 1980 presidential candidate, formulated it in his Four Laws of Ecology:

> Everything is connected to everything else.
> Everything must go somewhere.
> Nature knows best.
> There is no such thing as a free lunch.

Our treatment of mangroves has broken all of these laws. We have considered their removal to be of no consequence, only to find that we have lost fish nurseries, a marine nutrient input, a carbon sink, and a coastal shield. We have polluted or interfered with the hydrology of those that remain, and then been surprised when they slowly decay and die.

Like most countries with mangroves, Panama is in damage-con-trol mode, belatedly trying to stanch the loss of an undervalued re-source. It has strengthened its national protection policies and is committed to finding a path to conservation that doesn't leave sub-sistence coastal dwellers out in the cold. But when economic push comes to shove, as it has in Juan Díaz, it's hard not to see mangroves being the losers. They are just such tempting targets, residing as they do in prime coastal locations that are a developer's dream.

Ultimately, the solution to the mangrove dilemma may be to fight dollar with dollar. Value mangroves correctly, and their removal may prove unaffordable. This is the approach being taken by a new breed of economists, and I investigate it in the next and final chapter.

Chapter 14

A Mangrove's Worth

Our dominant economic model seeks and rewards
more versus better consumption, private versus public
wealth creation, man-made capital versus natural capital:
this is a triple whammy of destructive biases.
—PAVAN SUKHDEV, *study leader, The Economics of
Ecosystems and Biodiversity initiative, 2008*

*I*N 2007, A GROUP of eminent mangrove scientists warned that
if mangroves continue to disappear at the current rate of 1 to
2 percent per year, within 100 years they will be gone. Not extinct as individual species—there are enough protected stands to
guarantee their biological survival—but finished as providers of ecological services to the planet. As mangrove habitats become smaller
and more fragmented, a tipping point is reached. They can no longer
support the diversity of organisms that depend on them, or play
their ecological roles.

How do mangroves serve the planet? Let us count the ways—for
it turns out that mangroves are ecological Swiss Army knives, with a
blade for every purpose. Some services they offer by virtue of being
plants. They consume carbon dioxide, release oxygen, and create car-
bohydrates during photosynthesis. They form soil, store and sequester carbon, and cycle water and nutrients through the ecosystem.
These processes are fundamental to life on earth.

Other services arise from mangroves' location as trees of the tide. They buffer tropical coastlines from storm winds and waves. They capture and stabilize fine sediments. They act as biofilters, controlling nutrient runoff from the land and maintaining the quality of coastal waters on which other ecosystems such as coral reefs depend. They are also key suppliers of organic carbon to the oceans, dripfeeding a source of primary productivity to marine food webs. They provide nursery habitats and havens for marine organisms, and nesting and roosting space for birds. They are a source of pollen and nectar for bees and a source of fodder for browsing herbivores. Root to tip, they support great biodiversity.

The total value of mangrove ecosystem services has been estimated to be $10,000 per hectare per year ($4,000 per acre). In other words, when a hectare of mangroves is cut down, the environment loses $10,000 worth of annual support. Thus a 100-hectare (250-acre) shrimp farm constructed by clearing mangroves incurs an annual environmental deficit of $1 million—a cost that, if it were included in the price of the product, would take farmed shrimp off the fast-food menu.

It is precisely this point that incenses ecological economists: ecosystem services are not included in the market economy. They are referred to as externalities. The global free market thrives, say these economists, because externalities don't appear on the balance sheet; they are a debt to nature that is never paid. Or has not been until now.

Climate change, the bellwether issue of our time, has prompted a reevaluation. Since the Industrial Revolution—the commencement of the era of carbon profligacy—developed nations have racked up a huge debt with one particular ecosystem service: carbon dioxide storage in atmosphere and ocean. Now that bill is being collected. Warming, acidifying, rising oceans on the one hand; a warming, storming terrestrial climate on the other. It's like the landlord paying a visit, demanding 200 years of unpaid rent.

Carbon trading—the attempt to use market mechanisms to rescue the planet from CO_2 overload—requires precise accounting of carbon sources and sinks, and has brought the tools of economics to bear on the issue. A spin-off from this activity has been an effort to put a monetary value on other ecosystem services, including those provided by forests. In 1997, a team led by American ecological economist Robert Costanza estimated the total value of global ecosystem services, along with the natural capital stocks that produce them, to be between $16 trillion and $54 trillion, roughly one to three times more than the global gross national product at that time. The global economy was being subsidized at a ratio of between one-to-one and three-to-one by the environment.

In Costanza's calculation, mangroves had among the highest per-hectare value of any ecosystem—higher than coral reefs, continental shelves, and the open sea. Not bad at all for mosquito-infested wastelands.

Among the most studied services mangroves provide—because of their commercial importance—are those to fisheries. There is the nursery role, of course. One study found that 90 percent of commercial fish species in south Florida use mangrove estuaries as habitat during some stage of their life cycle. But other services, such as nutrient provision, water filtration, and uptake of agricultural chemicals, are also significant. A study of fish landings at thirteen sites in the Gulf of California recently found that yields were directly proportional to the length of coastline inhabited by mangroves. The researchers determined that the presence of mangroves was worth $37,500 per hectare ($15,000 per acre) per year for its fish-related services. This figure is 600 times the value the Mexican government places on mangrove land, which is acquired cheaply for tourism development and conversion to shrimp farms.

In 1994, a group of scientists estimated that for intensive shrimp farming to be environmentally sustainable, each farm would need an area of mangroves 35 to 190 times its size to provide fish meal, clean water, and brood stock, and to assimilate its wastes. For each calorie of edible shrimp protein produced by a shrimp farm, they estimated that approximately 295 calories of ecosystem work was required. Suppose each calorie of shrimp had a market price of one cent, and that the ecosystem services were valued at the same rate. In that case, the environment would be discounting the price of shrimp to the tune of $2.95 per calorie, or roughly $1,500 per pound of shrimp. Pink gold, indeed.

But this discount doesn't include the environmental liabilities of pond aquaculture that don't relate to mangroves, such as disruption of natural tidal flows, creek blockage, salinization of ground water, acidification of soil, release of toxic wastes and excess nutrients into coastal waters, overexploitation of wild larvae, and destructive by-catch of other marine life. None of these damages are accounted for in the market price of the farmed product; they are externalities—costs paid by the environment.

Also missing from the aquaculture pricing schedule (or the room rates of resorts built on mangrove land, or the price per pound of salt evaporated from ponds created by clearing mangroves, or any other product or enterprise that results from mangrove conversion) is the loss of coastal protection. No event highlighted this ecological role more profoundly than the Indian Ocean tsunami, which struck the day after Christmas 2004, killing an estimated 230,000 people in eleven countries. Along with the outpouring of grief that followed the tsunami was a sober counting of cost. The logic of allowing a country's mangrove barricades to be bulldozed for any and every purpose looked to be not just flawed but reprehensible. Like removing bolts from a bridge, destroying mangroves left coastlines structurally weakened.

To be sure, no coastal greenbelt, even one as interlocked in trunk, branch, and root as a mangrove forest, can quell the force of a 30-meter (100-foot) tsunami wave, but such extreme visitations are rare. For lesser waves—especially the surges generated by cyclones—mangroves have amply demonstrated their ability to protect and defend. But it took the catastrophic scale of the Indian Ocean tsunami to focus the world's attention on the human cost of mangrove loss.

Canadian ecological anthropologist Bradley B. Walters, who studies interactions between societies and the environment, had this to say:

> If past economic and environmental arguments for conserving mangroves were not viewed as synonymous with human security, it is perhaps only because we did not put a human face on those whose lives and livelihoods depend on these unique and valuable forests. Tragic as it was, the Asian Tsunami of 2004 gave us this human face and, in so doing, has redefined mangrove conservation as a human security concern.

Security, provisioning, the source of livelihoods—these are all services that mangroves provide to the coastal poor. For these people, the destruction of mangroves is not only an indirect ecological loss with outward rippling impacts, but also a direct social attack. Communities are fragmented. People are forced to migrate to the cities. Health and well-being suffer. But, like ecosystem damage, these social deficits are externalities that don't show up in the global economy.

Even if it were possible to put a price on the social services of mangroves, there are still other values that defy monetization. They are simply incommensurable with the market. Ecological economists speak of the intrinsic or non-use values of ecosystems, such as the aesthetic pleasure of the landscape or the sense of cultural identity they give to communities whose existence is embedded within them.

Some cultures imbue mangroves with sacred value. In the mythology of the Asmat people of Irian Jaya, a lonely Creator carves human-like figures from a mangrove root to keep him company. But his loneliness is not assuaged, so he cuts down a mangrove tree and makes its trunk into a drum. He starts drumming, and as he does the figures come to life and begin to dance. When today's Asmat carve their exquisite mangrove panels and canoe prows, each populated with ancestral figures, they are making a statement of identity and engaging in an act of worship.

Unravel the skein of values still further and you come to what ecological economists call the existence value of an ecosystem—its worth simply for *being there*. Many people cherish the existence of wild places for its own sake, and are troubled at the thought that present-day exploitation may rob future generations of the joy of natural places. Theodore Roosevelt's words, chiseled in stone in the entrance rotunda of the American Museum of Natural History, eloquently state the case for seeing nature as a bequest to those who follow us: "The nation behaves well if it treats the natural resources as assets which it must turn over to the next generation increased and not impaired in value."

How, then, are mangroves to be saved? As is the case with climate, a hefty dose of economic self-interest must play a role if the rainforests of the sea are to survive the ever-enlarging ecological footprint of *Homo sapiens*. The challenge, as globalization commentator Thomas Friedman puts it, is to make economic growth and environmentalism work together to produce "honest growth," where all the ecological services get counted.

But not everyone is in favor of putting a price tag on nature's services. Opponents argue that by adopting the value system of the marketplace, environmentalists are playing into the hands of commerce and selling nature short. If you're going to sup with the devil of monetarism, so the argument goes, you need a very long spoon.

I put the question to Harvard ecologist Aaron Ellison when I visited him at the Petersham campus in rural Massachusetts. Could we not find ourselves in the predicament Oscar Wilde described, where we know the price of everything and the value of nothing? "We're in the same situation with mangrove forests as we are with any other forest that we refer to as a 'natural resource,'" he said. "Error one is we call them a resource—so they're already disrespected. They're now something for us to consume and use instead of respect and live with. We don't call our next-door neighbors a resource, we call them neighbors and people, and we interact with them. If we thought of mangroves in the same way, we wouldn't be in the situation we are in today. But we call them a resource. And resources are meant to be exploited, extracted, turned into something that we humans want."

So it's partly a question of language—of how the issues are framed. The outspoken Spanish ecological economist Joan Martinez-Alier writes about this in his book *The Environmentalism of the Poor*. He argues that in resource conflicts such as mangroves versus shrimp farms, where the worlds of economy, ecology, and social justice collide, not all of the participants wish to be ensnared in a monetary paradigm. Where human life and human dignity are at stake, he writes, "the appropriate languages are livelihood, food security, human rights, community territorial rights, and not 'the internalization of externalities' in the price system, or the 'polluter pays principle,' or 'cost-benefit' analysis."

The reason mangrove forests have declined so precipitately is that the language of the marketplace has prevailed. Change comes when people are willing to listen to a different narrative and to embrace "honest growth." When I met Aaron Ellison, he had recently edited a review of the latest scientific literature on mangroves. Impressive as it was to see the wealth of research that was being conducted, it troubled him that the public remained little the wiser. "Somewhere gets walloped by a cyclone," he remarked. "Tens of thousands are left homeless because their coastal buffer was destroyed, and everyone seems surprised. What are we scientists not getting out? What are we not communicating? The scientific community produces papers by the thousand, but we're increasingly studying things that are disappearing. Somehow we have to get the message out that mangroves are more important than a golf course, a resort, shrimp three nights a week. Until people are willing to make that calculus, the forests are going to keep getting whittled away. We really do have to draw a line in the sand at some point and say, 'No more.'"

Ellison had been in Belize not long before we met. It was his first time back since he had studied mangroves there in the late 1990s. "Ten years ago there were no shrimp farms in Belize, and now thousands of hectares of mangroves have been converted to shrimp farms. There are sections of coast that have been turned into million-dollar resorts. And this in a country where everyone knows mangroves are important, that fish come from the mangroves. Talk to the taxi drivers. They know this. Belize promotes ecotourism. This is a country that has all the pieces in place, and then they chew their mangroves up for housing developments and shrimp ponds because it's a quicker source of revenue. There's a disconnect there that is very troubling."

My journey among mangroves has been an attempt to see beyond the disconnect—to find the links between mangroves and land and wildlife and people and livelihoods and coastal protection and fish nurseries . . . and all-you-can-eat shrimp buffets. To walk in a mangrove forest is to become aware of the interlocked worlds of land and sea, human and wild. The egret roosting in the treetops in snowy splendor. The fiddler crab waving on the stream bank. The barracuda snooping through the root cloisters. The cockle collector probing in the mud. And, undergirding them all, the silent, fervid productivity of the forest.

Standing within the green pavilion, I, too, feel linked to the whole. I imagine a carbon atom in my exhaled breath being fixed in a mangrove leaf that one day drops to the sediment, is macerated by a mud crab, drifts offshore in the organic soup, and is built into a head of staghorn coral that, in twenty years' time, I snorkel past and admire with my grandchild.

Mangroves are such a small part of the biosphere. They comprise less than half a percent of the world's forests, and occupy only one-thousandth of the land area of the planet. But they matter. They matter to organisms and ecological processes on land and sea, and they matter to millions of people. *El manglar es nuestra casa*—the mangrove is our home. It is a home worth protecting.

Author's Note

EW ZEALANDERS are used to looking at the world from a distance. Where I live, in Auckland, mangroves are nearing their southernmost geographical limit. We have only one species of mangrove in New Zealand, and in some estuaries it grows not much taller than a garden shrub. So I look at the world of mangroves from the margins. And perhaps I look more enviously than someone living in Southeast Asia or Central America, in the mangrove heartlands, might do.

Nevertheless, I have been aware of the trees of the tide for as long as I can remember. As a child, I used to pick up their plump green propagules off the beach, where they washed up by the thousands. Each was an eight-page leaf book that I pretended to read. When I was older I would paddle a kayak or row a dinghy into the mangroves at high tide to watch shoals of yellow-eyed mullet glide through the warren of underwater trunks and roots, and pink jellyfish undulate against the press of the tide. I trailed my fingers in the algal soup that bathes the trees and heard the plop of ripe propagules falling into the water.

Or I walked into the forests at low tide, when the rivulets drain and the mudflats breathe again. I listened for the pistol-crack report of snapping shrimp, and watched whelks wave their trunklike proboscēs as they crawled across the sticky surface, following scent trails to carrion. At countless burrow entrances mud crabs scuttled in and out, cleaning and repairing their homes after the tide's incursion. I watched white-faced herons at the water's edge pause in midstride, dagger bills poised to stab—the embodiment of Steinbeck's "stalking quiet murder." Each step took me ankle- or knee-deep into squelching sludge that changed from tea-brown to cement-gray to coal-black the deeper I sank.

It was this longstanding fascination with a little-known habitat that prompted me in 2005 to propose a mangrove story to *National Geographic*. The magazine accepted, and I traveled to Africa, Asia, and Latin America to report on mangrove communities far richer than those I knew back home. I expected to tell a story of mystic places, exotic species, and unique customs—all in danger of disappearance. I found these things, but what struck me most was the social cost of mangrove loss. I saw impoverished communities battling powerful industrial interests for the preservation of their forests, and I realized that for these people mangroves are not an incidental background to their lives but a vital, sustaining presence. When they fight for the mangroves, they fight for their own future.

Their plight began the journey that has led to this book—a journey made possible, and unforgettable, by many people in many countries. My sincere thanks go to those who guided me: in Bangladesh, Rubáiyát Mansur Mowgli and Elisabeth Fahrni Mansur of The Guide Tours; in Tanzania, Rose Hogan; in Malaysia, Ong Jin Eong; in Eritrea, Gordon Sato and Simon Tecleab; in Panama, Rosabel Miró, Karl Kaufmann, and Ilka (Candy) Feller; in Florida, Andy From, Tom Smith, and Robin Lewis; in Ecuador, Edgar Lemos and Pedro Ordinola; in Bimini, Grant Johnson, Matt Potenski, and the staff and volunteers of Shark Lab.

Special thanks are due to Elaine Corets, the Latin American coordinator of the Mangrove Action Project. As well as guiding and interpreting for me in Ecuador and Brazil, she planned the itinerary, coordinated the logistics, and introduced me to people who have been marginalized by the shrimp industry and who fight to preserve the mangrove remnant. Elaine has been an unflagging collaborator in this entire project.

Many others gave their time and expertise: Aaron Ellison of Harvard; Jeovah Meireles, geography professor and tireless promoter of mangrove conservation in Brazil; the Galdino brothers of Caravelas; and Cecília Mello, whose anthropological study of the town's reactions to the COOPEX shrimp farm proposal I found so illuminating (and who shared with me a motivating line from Brazilian author Clarice Lispector: "For he had an experience, a pencil and a paper, he had the intention and the wish—nobody ever had more than that"); Samuel Gruber, founder of the Bimini Biological Field Station, and his wife, Marie, who welcomed me into their Miami home; Verónica Yépez of the Ecuadorian mangrove advocacy organization C-CONDEM; Barnabas Mgweno of IUCN Tanzania; Alfredo Quarto, cofounder of the Mangrove Action Project; and John Walsby, a New Zealand naturalist whose enthusiasm for mangrove ecology first opened my eyes to the biological richness of the rainforests of the sea.

Fieldwork in the Americas was made possible by grants from the Overbrook Foundation and the Rainforest Information Service. I thank both organizations for their support, as I do *National Geographic*, which made possible my first period of field research.

I am grateful to Todd Baldwin and Emily Davis of Island Press for shepherding the text through to publication, and to a former Island Press editor, Jonathan Cobb, for championing the project at the outset. These are difficult times for publishers, and Island's willingness to take on a book about a less-than-mainstream subject is salutary. I tip my hat to Island's president, Chuck Savitt, for his commitment to disseminate knowledge that, as the New York Times noted recently, "would otherwise languish unshared."

A word to my wife, Cheryl, whom, fittingly, I met in the mangroves of Fiji thirty-three years ago during a university marine biology course. We were observing fiddler crabs, as I recall. During the months in which I was writing this book, sequestered like a good little carbon atom from the oxidative distractions to which I fall so easily prey, I was not an especially interactive partner. "Honey, I'm back."

The question arises (or at least I hope it does): What can we do to help reverse mangrove decline? I suspect that our greatest contribution, as individuals and communities, is to be responsible consumers, aware that our economic choices have global consequences. We can demand that suppliers and purveyors demonstrate that the seafood we eat comes from sustainable sources, and we can vote with our palates and pockets if it doesn't.

Furthermore, we can insist that food be not just ecologically sound but socially fair—to the extent that fairness is possible in an unequal world. We can refuse to give our business to companies that are known to trade in the marginalization of the poor.

In thinking about all that we stand to lose if mangroves disappear—the extinction of the world's only saltwater tiger, prowling the Sundarbans labyrinth, the loss of lofty carbon storehouses and resilient storm barriers, the emptying of the "supermarkets of the poor"—I draw hope from the famous words of Margaret Mead: "Never doubt that a small group of thoughtful, committed citizens can change the world. Indeed, it is the only thing that ever has."

Further Reading

General

Aquatic Botany 89 (2) (special mangrove issue). 2008.

Field, Colin. 1995. *Journey among Mangroves*. Okinawa, Japan: International Society for Mangrove Ecosystems.

Food and Agriculture Organization of the United Nations. 2007. *The World's Mangroves 1980–2005*, Forestry Paper 153. Rome: FAO.

Journal of Sea Research 59 (1–2) (special mangrove issue). 2008.

MacNae, William. 1968. "A General Account of the Fauna and Flora of Mangrove Swamps in the Indo-West Pacific Region." *Advances in Marine Biology* 6: 73–270.

Mastaller, Michael. 1997. *Mangroves: The Forgotten Forest Between Land and Sea*. Kuala Lumpur, Malaysia: Tropical Press.

Saenger, Peter. 2002. *Mangrove Ecology, Silviculture and Conservation*. Dordrecht, Netherlands: Kluwer Academic Publishers.

Spalding, Mark, Mami Kainuma, and Lorna Collins. 2010. *World Atlas of Mangroves*. Stirling, VA: Earthscan Publications.

Tomlinson, P. B. 1986. *The Botany of Mangroves*. Cambridge: Cambridge University Press.

Ecological role of mangroves

Alongi, Daniel. 2009. *The Energetics of Mangrove Forests*. New York: Springer Science.

Luther, David, and Russell Greenberg. 2009. "Mangroves: A Global Perspective on the Evolution and Conservation of Their Terrestrial Vertebrates." *BioScience* 59: 602–12.

Coastal buffer role of mangroves

Barbier, Edward. 2006. "Natural Barriers to Natural Disasters: Replanting Mangroves After the Tsunami." *Frontiers in Ecology and the Environment* 4 (3): 124–31.

Walters, Bradley B. 2008. "Mangrove Forests and Human Security." *CAB Reviews* 3 (64): 1–9.

Mangroves, shrimp, and people

Bergquist, Daniel. 2008. "Colonised Coasts: Aquaculture and Energy Flows in the World System: Cases from Sri Lanka and the Philippines." *Geografiska regionstudier* 77: 192 pp.

Food and Agriculture Organization of the United Nations. 2009. *The State of the World Fisheries and Aquaculture 2008.* Rome: FAO.

MacKenzie Jr., Clyde. 2001. "The Fisheries for Mangrove Cockles, *Anadara* spp., from Mexico to Peru, with Descriptions of Their Habitats and Biology, the Fishermen's Lives, and the Effects of Shrimp Farming." *Marine Fisheries Review* 63 (1): 1–39.

Martinez-Alier, Joan. 2002. *The Environmentalism of the Poor: A Study of Ecological Conflicts and Valuation.* Cheltenham, UK: Edward Elgar.

Primavera, J. H. 1997. "Socio-economic Impacts of Shrimp Culture." *Aquaculture Research* 28: 815–27.

Websites

Bimini Biological Field Station (Shark Lab),
    http://www6.miami.edu/sharklab/index.html

Center for the Advancement of the Steady State Economy,
    http://steadystate.org/learn/blog/

Lewis Environmental Services (ecological mangrove restoration),
    http://www.mangroverestoration.com

Mangrove Action Project, http://www.mangroveactionproject.org

Manzanar Project, http://www.tamu.edu/ccbn/dewitt/manzanar
    /default.htm

Smithsonian Mangrove Biocomplexity project,
    http://www.serc.si.edu/labs/animal_plant_interaction/index.aspx

US Geological Survey National Wetlands Center,
    http://www.nwrc.usgs.gov

World Wildlife Fund Shrimp Dialogue,
    http://www.worldwildlife.org/what/globalmarkets/aquaculture
    /dialogues-shrimp.html

Index

About Island Press